Sunlight on the Sea

Reflecting on Reflections

DAVID E. COOPER

CONTENTS

1 THE SUN AND THE SEA

'There's no escaping from it. Incessant gleams of light flash from th[e] mirror-like expanse' of 'the unharvested sea'. 'Even when unperceived by the senses', Norman Douglas continues, 'among squalid tenements or leafy uplands, they will find you out and follow, like some all-pervading, inevitable melody'.

The author of *South Wind*, *Siren Land* and other homages to the Mediterranean and its islands is not alone in his inescapable fascination with the sun's effects on the surface of the sea. It was shared, for example, by the literary émigrés to the Mediterranean from England and 'the gothic North', as W.H. Auden called it, during the twentieth century – Auden himself, D.H. Lawrence, Anthony Burgess, Lawrence Durrell, Nicholas Monsarrat and others. They were themselves following the trails of earlier writers, like Edward Lear, in search of Keats' 'beaker full of the warm South'.

I am among the willing victims to those 'incessant gleams' of sunlight that 'flash' from the sea. Like Douglas, they follow me to very different places and ask to be refreshed.

But why? Why should the experience of sunlight reflected by the surface of water, of the sea especially, be of significance to a person? Why should it be inescapable and pervade his or her life?

This book is one person's attempt to address these questions – to understand the place in his life of a kind of experience, but in the hope, naturally, that his words illuminate matters for other victims. I am writing these particular words on the small island of Gozo, just south of Sicily. This afternoon, I shall walk across a garrigue to the edge of a great white cliff that affords - on this warm, spring day - the sight of a sea that sparkles. I would like to communicate why this sight matters to me, and in a way that does not render my experience eccentric, but of a kind that has a significant place in the lives of many readers.

The book is not about the sun or the sea taken in isolation from one another. Its theme is sun-and-sea, the sun on the sea. There exists an affinity, or intimacy, between sun and sea, and in several different respects. The novelist, Llewelyn Powys, was right to observe that, for millennia, 'the sunlight and the sea and the masterless winds have held tryst together'. By including the wind in this tryst, he draws attention to the physical processes in which sunlight and the sea combine. Heat from the sun, and sunspots, cause winds that then distribute heat through the currents they produce. Global warming allows jelly fish, blown northwards, to survive in waters once too cold for them. A complex of physical relations between sun and sea enables surfers to practice their art. As a poetic champion of this art and sport explains, 'the wind speaks the message of the sun to the sea, and the sea transmits it on through waves'.

Long before meteorologists, oceanographers and surfers worked out the physical interactions between sun and sea, however, the two had been brought together in myth and religion. It was when, in the form of mist, the gods 'drew forth the sun that was hidden in the sea', relates the Rig Veda, that they 'caused the worlds to swell' and established 'order and truth'. The main Shinto deity, Amaterasu, is a sun goddess 'born of water'. She had to be induced to leave a cave, into which she had retreated, so that the light and warmth required for spring to begin and the crops to grow could be restored. The ruse was to place a mirror in front of the cave so that the goddess would step outside to admire her own radiance. Human beings, it seems, must honour and humour the sun if it is to serve their needs.

Sun and sea are indissolubly linked in the Greek myth of Helios and its many variants across the world, in Peru and Chile for example. Helios was the Titan who carried the sun across the sky in a chariot, descending each evening into the ocean whose currents then carried him eastward to start another day.

Sun and sea are in league, too, in the legend of Odysseus. In Sicily, the hero's companions eat the sacred cattle of Helios' father, Hyperion. Their punishment is to perish in the straits of Messina between a rock and a whirlpool, Scylla and Charybdis. Odysseus manages to survive, as he also does on a later occasion when Poseidon, the sea-god, whips up a storm in revenge for the blinding of his son, Polyphemus, the Cyclops whose eye was an emblem of the sun.

The sea aids and abets the sun, as well, in the story of Icarus. The young man's hubris in attempting to fly close to the sun is punished by the melting of the wax that fastened his wings. Icarus falls to his death in the sea that awaits him below.

These days 'sun worship' is more apt to evoke images of summer holidays - or winter breaks in the tropics - than of religious rituals. Perhaps the metaphor should be taken seriously: maybe the modern sun-seeking tourist is paying a kind of homage and acting out a perennial human urge. Scott Fitzgerald likened the beach at Antibes, on which his fellow Americans prostrated themselves, to a prayer mat. It's interesting that Fitzgerald's example is a beach, for it is where sun and sea meet that recreational sun worship is most conspicuously practised. If the metaphor of sun worship is a serious one, so is that of sun bathing. It is possible, of course, to enjoy the sun in deserts or valleys far from the sea. Possible, too, to enjoy grey, murky waters shielded from the sun by leaden clouds. But it is on the beach that seekers of the sun and lovers of the sea primarily converge.

This has not always been so. Even as late as Scott Fitzgerald's 1920s jazz age, many of the growing number of people heading for the beach needed an excuse for their indulgence. The type provided, for example, by naturist cults that preached the medical, spiritual and 'vital' benefits of sun and sea. In a book of 1889 by Edward Carpenter – a utopian socialist and advocate of homoeroticism – 'saturation with sunlight' was a way of being 'cured' of a 'civilization' guilty of cramping body and soul alike.

Today's sunbathers feel no need to provide justifications. 'Sun' and 'sea', followed shortly by 'sand' and 'sex', comprise the mantra of beach holidays. If any excuse is offered, it is only for exposing unprotected skin to ultra-violet radiation.

Described in myth and in science, enjoyed by surfers and sunbathers, the affinity of sun and sea is also represented or evoked in art. Looking out towards the Aegean from the Acropolis on a spring day in 1903, the Danish composer, Carl Nielsen, was moved to write an overture that he named after Helios, the sun-bearing Titan. The music emerges, like the sun itself, from 'silence and darkness', and proceeds to depict the risen sun as it 'wanders on its golden way' and finally 'sinks quietly into the sea'.

If sun and sea is an occasional subject for music, it is a regular one for painting. In 1807, J.W.M. Turner painted a picture of fishermen cleaning and selling fish by the shore. Its title, 'Sun rising through vapour', might apply, one art historian noted, to half of Turner's works. The list of painters who, like Turner, accepted the challenge, or experienced a compulsion, to depict the relationship between sun and water is a long one. It might begin with Van Gogh, Monet, Munch, Matisse and Hockney.

A main concern of these painters – to render reflections in water - returns us to the theme of this book. Sometimes – as in the case of 'Sun rising through vapour' or Eduard Munch's gigantic mural, 'The Sun' – these are the direct reflections of the sun on the surface of the sea. Sometimes, as with Claude Monet's painting of the harbour at Le Havre, 'Impression, Sunrise', they are the reflections of objects, like boats, illuminated by the sun. Either way, such works convey the feeling that the sun, to be properly appreciated, needs to be viewed via its reflections in water. (Perhaps a message of the Amaterasu story is that, to be rightly admired, the sun must be seen in a kind of mirror.)

Some of the best-known musical evocations of sun and sea are tonal portraits of reflections in water. Claude Debussy disliked being called a musical Impressionist, but works like 'Poissons d'or' might have been soundtracks to paintings of reflections, including the one by Monet of Le Havre that gave to the Impressionist movement its name. One of Debussy's most effective pieces, the first of his *Images*, is called 'Reflets dans l'eau'. For me, it is difficult, too, to hear quicksilver miniatures by Maurice Ravel, like 'Jeux d'eau', without visualising sparkling lights on the surface of water.

John Ruskin doubted that art could represent the sea and its reflections with complete success. Painting the sea is like 'trying to paint a soul ... [something] beyond the power of man'. But he also thought that painters of genius, above all Turner, could render the sea better than anyone else. Better, certainly, than philosophers and other word-mongers. 'There is more in Turner's painting of water surfaces than any philosophy of reflection ... can account for'. His painting records a 'wonder' that defies explanation. Ruskin, I hope, is too pessimistic, for what the present book attempts could be called 'a philosophy of reflection', or perhaps 'a phenomenology of reflection' – an enquiry into the significance of people's experience of sunlight on the surface of the sea. I want to understand, for example, why and how, for Arthur Schopenhauer, 'the incredible beauty of the reflection of objects in water' was the 'most perfect and pure of our perceptions', and the one that brought him most pleasure (in an admittedly rather pleasure-free life).

The book is not a poem, but it engages in what T.S. Eliot took the aim of poems to be – 'a raid on the inarticulate', a riposte to 'undisciplined squads of emotion'. A book, even a poetic one, cannot, of course, communicate an experience of reflections in water in the manner of a Turner canvas or a piano piece by Ravel. But it might do something to salvage the experience from the realm of the inexplicable to which Ruskin consigned it.

I speak of *the* experience, but there is, of course, boundless variety in the experience of sun on sea. The 'moods ... of the face of the sea', noted one close observer, Rachel Carson, 'vary from hour to hour'.

How the sun's reflection on the surface of water is experienced depends on different kinds of factor. On the atmospheric conditions and time of day, for instance. As he sailed around Sicily on to Sardinia, D.H. Lawrence recorded the evening sun's 'lovely strong winey warmth' glowing 'golden over a deep-blue sea'. At dawn, by contrast, he reports a 'delighted' sea, like 'sequins shaking', beneath an 'unfathomably clear sky'.

Experience varies, too, according to the position and other aspects of the observer. Light bouncing from the sea will look one way to a person perched on a cliff, quite another to a swimmer whose eyes are only an inch above the waves. Spots of light on the surface look different when you half-close your eyes or squint: they begin to dance like Lawrence's sparkling sequins.

Context matters, too – the presence or absence, say, of bouncing boats or swooping birds. Henri Matisse – for whom wintering in Paris was 'demi-suicide' – describes how, on a visit to Apataki atoll, it is the experience of sea, sky, coconut palms and fish in combination that makes it 'radiant' and 'precious'.

Connoisseurs of sun on sea, like Lawrence and Matisse, will draw many more, and finer-grained, distinctions among their experiences than the few I've sketched. They will differ, as well, on which experiences are most precious or significant for them. For some, the waves should be choppy, for others gently rolling. For some, the sun should be deep amber, for others pale lemon. Many people will not be sure, nor perhaps care, which experiences they enjoy most. They may face the happy dilemma of the hermit, encountered by the Countess of Blessington on Ischia in 1839, who didn't know whether the water around the island 'appears more lovely when sparkling in the light beams of the morning, or when the sun sinks into the sea, casting its red light over the scene'.

The sea indeed has many moods and it belongs to the fascination and significance of the sun's effects upon it that so many of these may be appreciated by one and the same person. The diversity of these pleasures seems itself to be an object of pleasure. The ephemeral character of experiences of sun on sea appears to enhance their value.

The sun's reflection in the sea is not, of course, the only form of light reflected in water. Monet's pond at Giverny reflects the sun as much as the sea at Le Havre, and Californian swimming pools, not only the waves off Malibu, do the reflecting in Hockney's paintings. Lakes, writes Emerson, also transmit 'ineffable glances' from 'sun set clouds' – and from stars and moon as well. If the sea records 'the sun's great gestures and pressions' so, Lawrence adds, it can 'take the moon as in a sieve and sift her flake by flake'. Harbour lights, Japanese lanterns and neon-lit signs also get reflected by water.

In the chapters that follow, these other types of reflection are not excluded. The focus, though, is on what seems to me to be the richest form of reflection – the sun's effect on the surface of the sea. This is the form that has most inspired the spirit and has most to tell us about life and its enhancement.

It won't matter much, when reading these chapters, which images or memories, to recall Norman Douglas' words, most persistently find you out and follow you about like an inevitable melody. In my own case, the sights that resonate most are those from an elevated point on a small island – Lindisfarne, say, or Gozo – that take in a surrounding, mildly agitated sea glinting beneath a bright, but not cruelly glaring sun. Readers are free to substitute their own most vivid or poignant visions as they ask whether my exploration of such experiences rings true for them.

2 LIFE AND ILLUMINATION

Our question is this: why should experience of the sun reflected by the sea be of significance to people? An experience that follows them around and beckons them? Why is the sight of sun on sea one that many people don't simply enjoy, but feel a need for? The very short answer is: it enhances life. But this answer is not only too cryptic, it is liable to mislead. For I have something more complex in mind by 'life' than most writers who have made connections between life, sun and sea.

I drew attention, earlier, to the cultish enthusiasm for sun and sea – among naturists, health fetishists and others – that spread early in the twentieth century. This enthusiasm invoked and tapped into a wider 'vitalist' ideology. The goal of people's lives, it was proclaimed, was life itself – the cultivation of an *élan vital* coursing through everything and able to overcome the cramping, desiccating constraints of modern civilization.

Life, in this sense, was typically pitted against rationality, science and social convention. The great 'struggle', wrote a Spanish philosopher of the period, is between 'reason and life'. For D.H. Lawrence, 'the intellect is only a bridle ... All I want is to answer to my blood, direct, without the fribbling intervention of mind, morals, or what not'.

Lawrence, of course, was uncompromising in his search and love for places where sun and sea came together. He was also an admirer of Friedrich Nietzsche, who had already forged a close association between life, sun and sea. 'Like the sun', declares Nietzsche's Zarathustra, 'I love life and all deep seas'. It is 'like the morning sun' that Zarathustra emerges from his cave – in the manner of Amaterasu – all 'glowing and strong'.

The author of *Sons and Lovers* was to eroticise this Nietzschean connection between life, sun and sea in his succinctly titled short story, 'Sun'. Seeking an Italian escape from people, including her husband, who are 'unelemental ... unsunned ... like graveyard worms', Juliet has fantasies of making love to a peasant who would be a 'procreative sun-bath' to her, and indeed of 'mating' with the sun itself. Through 'the mysterious power' of the sun, writes Lawrence, life again begins to throb through Juliet. 'I can't go back', she explains to her pleading husband, 'I can't go back on the sun'.

I don't want to belittle the enhancement of life emphasised by vitalists. Enervation can be disabling. Vigour and energy are preconditions of a full life. Nietzsche was right to scold philosophy and religion for ignoring what he ironically calls 'the little things' - 'nutrition, place, climate and recreation'.

So to the degree that experience and enjoyment of sun and sea tones people up and invigorates them, it enhances life. And only an unappealingly ascetic conception of the good life would begrudge people the erotic glow felt on the skin as they emerge from the sea beneath a warming sun.

But when Nietzsche goes on to insist that 'the little things' are 'the most basic concerns of life itself', and are 'inconceivably more important' than what philosophy and religion regard as important, the reader pauses. For all its attractive bounce and élan, life as it is understood by Lawrence and the vitalists is impoverished. A good human life – one that is full, rounded, flourishing – is not lived in opposition to 'intellect, mind and morals'. It is not doomed to a perpetual 'struggle between reason and life' itself.

So, if the experience of sun and sea is life-enhancing, its contribution is to life in a more nuanced, more complex and less athletic sense than the one urged by vitalists.

This richer notion of life is found, with significant variations, in many ancient traditions of wisdom. The central focus of ancient ethics – in

India and China, as well as Greece – was the good life for a human being. This kind of ethical concern is sometimes called 'virtue ethics', the virtues being those dispositions of a person, those qualities of 'character', that contribute towards a good life. The point of the label is partly to distinguish this ancient emphasis from more modern forms of moral concern, at least in the West. Here, in recent centuries, the main focus has not been the person, but action. What makes an action right? Its contribution to overall utility, its accordance with divine command, its status as a duty, its endorsement by society – or what? For the ancients, such questions are secondary to the essential issue of the nature of the good life.

'Virtues' is not an especially happy word to have to use, redolent as it is of a particular set of earnest character traits admired by the Victorians. So it is important in what follows to hear the word in its older sense, as referring to those aspects of character - those tendencies to act and to feel and to speak – that need to be cultivated if a person's life is to go well. The Greek and Chinese terms often translated by the word 'virtues' are more literally rendered as 'excellences' or 'powers'. Certainly some of the virtues I shall be identifying do not belong on standard lists of the moral virtues familiar in the West.

In the ancient traditions I have in mind, there is always a figure, an exemplar, who serves as a model of the virtues, of a flourishing and fulfilled human life. The Confucian 'consummate person', for example, or the Daoist 'sage', or the 'enlightened' Buddhist, or the Greek 'eudaimon' (sometimes translated as 'the happy person', but better rendered as someone whose life goes well and accords with the purpose of human existence). These figures are by no means the same. The enlightened Buddhist is a more austere figure than the Greek eudaimon and less socially engaged than the consummate Confucian. What unites them is their status, in the different traditions, as exemplars of the good life.

But not just this: for, among the traditions there is also agreement on the main ingredients of the lives of these exemplary figures. These ingredients are the famous triad of truth, goodness, and beauty. The life of the exemplar is marked by an understanding of the way of things, by virtue, and by the appreciation and manifestation of beauty.

It is important, straightaway, to emphasise that, in these traditions, the three ingredients are not independent of one another. They are not the separate, unrelated items that they are treated as being in modern Western thought. Truth, goodness and beauty, for the ancients, form a unity.

Understanding and virtue presuppose one another: there is, as Socrates said, 'a unity of knowledge and virtue'. The vicious person is lacking in understanding. The person whom the Greeks called 'fully' virtuous – or to whom Daoists attribute 'profound *de* [virtue]' – does not simply do and say the right things, but does so on the basis of understanding the world and human nature aright. What makes a life an exemplary one is, in part, its harmony with the way of things as truly understood. Conversely, a person cannot be said genuinely to have this understanding unless it is manifested in virtuous behaviour. According to the Buddha, the 'noble truths' he announced have not been fully internalised by someone who fails to act compassionately. Wisdom and compassion are inseparable.

Beauty, too, in these traditions is inseparable from goodness. According to context, the Greek word *kalon* – like parallel terms in ancient Chinese and Sanskrit – may be translated either by 'beauty' or by 'good'. This testifies not to the ambiguity of the terms, but to an intimacy once experienced between what we now distinguish as aesthetic and ethical appreciation. In Confucian writings, the importance is often stressed of making ritual beautiful if it is fulfil its aim of bringing people together in their exercise of communal and familial virtues. Where aesthetic accomplishments, such as grace and decorum, leave off and moral ones begin was, for the Confucian an idle question. And so it was for the thinkers of India and Greece. When the Buddha asks 'What is beauty for the monk?', his answer refers to a list of virtues, including self-restraint, while another Buddhist text speaks of a woman who has been 'made beautiful by reason of the true doctrine'. And for Plato, beauty is, as it were, the attractive face of goodness, what makes goodness magnetic.

To understand the relevance of these ancient traditions to our theme of sun and sea, we need to attend to a further aspect they share. Although they are often presented in contemporary histories of ideas as systematic theories, these ancient dispensations were essentially practical, even therapeutic, in aim. Their purpose was not to instil people's minds with doctrine, but to transform their lives. For Plato, the true task of education is not the accumulation of information, but a reorientation of the soul in the direction of the good. Both the Buddha and Confucius were impatient with 'unprofitable' questions that have no bearing on the alleviation of suffering or the promotion of harmonious social relations. Buddhism and Shinto have been respectively described as a religion 'without beliefs' and 'spirituality without agenda'. These descriptions may be exaggerated, but they usefully draw attention to the priority of practice over the articulation of theory in these religions.

It cannot, in fact, have been the ambition of the teachers of these dispensations to articulate a complete account of reality, since they shared the conviction that there is mystery or ineffability in the nature of reality. 'The *dao* that can be spoken of', announces the opening line of the *Daodejing*, 'is not the constant *dao*', while a later chapter reminds us that 'those who talk about [the *dao*] do not know', and those who know don't talk about it. Plato fears it would make him 'ridiculous' to attempt to describe the 'Form of the Good' – the supreme Form responsible for all other Forms that structure the world: 'we should forget about trying to define' it. Reality as such, remarks the founder of the Sōtō sect of Zen Buddhism, Dōgen, is 'something ineffable' – something 'inaccesible to discursive thought', as it is put in one of the Mahayana texts on which he draws.

The aim of the ancient dispensations is not to equip people with bodies of doctrine or theory, but to attune them to the world, to cultivate experience of truth, virtue and beauty – the triple dimensions of the good life. Daoism, Buddhism and the other traditions mentioned seek to render these dimensions present to people, to give them salience in consciousness and practice. To use a term that is ubiquitous in East Asian traditions, the aim is to put a person 'on the way' – one that leads to, or indeed *is*, the good life.

That the aim is the cultivation of experience and practice, not the transmission of doctrine, explains the presence in the literature of these traditions of those exemplary figures alluded to earlier – the sages, consummate persons and others who embody the good life. These figures *show* in their lives what cannot be *said*, and by placing confidence in them and emulating their practice a person may approximate to the good life that they exemplify. This is why, in all the traditions mentioned, it is emphasised that the exemplary figure should be charismatic, exerting a magnetism that will draw other men and women to follow a path. Here lies the reason for what might seem to modern readers an obsession with, say, the demeanour and comportment of the Confucian gentleman or with the bodily radiance of Gautama, the Buddha.

Emulation of exemplary figures is not the only means of cultivating the desired experiences and practices. A striking feature of the ancient literatures is their deployment of imagery, metaphors, anecdotes and other rhetorical devices to help attune people to the dimensions of the good life. What cannot be said may be evoked or intimated through such devices. It is through allegories that Plato's *Republic* conveys a sense of the Form of the Good, and through stories of craftsmen, fishermen and others that Zhuangzi provides a feel for the spontaneous, natural life advocated in Daoism.

Here, at last, we reconnect with the topic of this book. For, there are no images, metaphors, allegories and anecdotes that are more prominent in these ancient literatures than those inspired by the phenomenon of illumination. Many of these specifically invoke the sun, water and reflections – often all three together.

The source of the 'reality and being' of things, says Plato, is 'beyond comprehension', but we are given a sense of it by a comparison with its 'child', the sun. As the sun nourishes material things and illuminates them so that they are visible to us, so the Form of the Good is responsible for 'intelligible' things, such as numbers, and for our ability to grasp them. And just as people emerging from a cave must get used to the bright light by looking at reflections in water before 'feasting their eyes' on the sun, so a vision of the source of reality requires an ascent from ignorance through lucid experience of the world whose source it is.

In several East Asian schools of Buddhism, such as Shingon in Japan, the 'Buddha-nature' that is deemed responsible for there being anything at all is compared to a 'great sun' that 'constantly emits great beams' that light up the world and the mind. Not only things, but 'all virtuous activities come from the Buddha's light'. The world is a 'quicksilver universe', a 'luminous flow' in which things 'interpenetrate' and reflect one another, like the waves on the surface of the sea. Indeed, it is this mutual reflection that provides the Buddhist schools with a metaphor for how, despite its apparent diversity, the world is a unity. Dewdrops, Dōgen explains, are many, but it is the same world that is reflected in each of them.

Daoism has been called 'the watercourse way', and certainly water provides the 'root' metaphor for both the *dao* itself and for the life of the sage who emulates the *dao*. Like a stream, the life of someone 'on the way' is a spontaneous, unforced flow that gently overcomes obstacles and reaches its destination. The mind of the sage is also compared to the surface of water. Properly to reflect the way of things, the mind must be calm, but not so still as to become turbid. Clarity requires vital activity on the sage's part: the mind, Zhuangzi explains, must flow like water, so that stillness and motion combine like the powers of yin and yang.

I could go on providing further illustrations of the metaphors, allegories and other rhetorical invocations of illumination that are employed in the ancient traditions. But those I have given are sufficient to show that, for the thinkers who forged and refined these traditions, experience of the sun and sea – or more generally, of light reflected in water – may be drawn upon in meditations on the good life. How this experience is interpreted - and in pursuit of what conceptions of truth, goodness and beauty – this will vary from tradition to tradition. In the chapters that follow, I shall often draw on these traditions, not because I identify with any one of them, but as inspirations, nevertheless, for my own proposals concerning the significance for life of the experience of sun and sea.

3 BEAUTY AND RADIANCE

Once again I look down onto the sea from a high cliff at the edge of a Maltese garrigue. The water, mildly agitated by an easterly wind, is azure close to shore, blue-black further out. Everywhere its surface sparkles. It is beautiful.

So there is this obvious connection between the sun on the sea and one dimension of the good life: the sun's reflection in the sea is beautiful. In Plato's idiom, it partakes in beauty. By beginning with beauty, I am in fact following Plato's lead. In several of his dialogues, he argues that if people are to be motivated to pursue goodness and truth, they must first experience beauty. This is because it is beauty that attracts. A virtue like justice or a geometrical theorem is too dry, as it were, to be enticing unless we are able to recognize its place within an order of reality that is beautiful.

Hence the famous 'ascent' that Socrates recalls the priestess Diotima having once described to him, and which he then describes to his fellow-diners in Plato's philosophical drama, *The Symposium*. Beginning with admiration, or love, for the beautiful body of a boy, the cultivated Greek man ascends to an appreciation of the symmetry and harmony, not only of physical things, but of laws, social institutions, mathematical systems, and much else. The ascent is from 'physical beauty to moral beauty', and beyond – to 'the beauty of knowledge'.

You don't have to be a Platonist to see sense in Plato's strategy of beginning with an immediately attractive experience of beauty and then seeking the meaning of this attraction by tracing the paths that lead from it to other areas of the good life. And we can, nearly all of us, agree on the beauty of light's reflection in water. It is this, of course, that has drawn painters, composers and writers – Turner, Debussy,

Lawrence and the rest – to devote themselves to rendering the phenomenon.

But the beauty of reflections in water hardly comes as big news. And, anyway, countless other phenomena – flowers, snowflakes, goldfinches, panthers - have a beauty that immediately attracts. How, we need to ask, might the beauty of sun and sea be distinctive in its significance?

A point worth making is that sun and sea often provide the context – the frame, backdrop, ambience – for things to show their beauty. Brightly coloured boats in a harbour, a white classical temple on the coast, an off-shore Shinto *torii* need the help of a sparkling blue sea to look their best. André Gide – another Nietzsche-inspired twentieth-century rhapsodist of sun and sea – notes how, at Sorrento, a 'grey sky had robbed the whole scene of its magic', including a hotel garden by the sea that now just looked 'dreary'. The Californian gardens designed by Thomas Church, perched above the Pacific, only become vibrant when the sun plays on a sea that also serves as borrowed scenery for their Hockney-like swimming pools. Even Gertrude Jekyll's modest garden on Lindisfarne looks resplendent on those rare sunny days when it is seen surrounded by the usually more sullen North Sea. It is not just gardens, of course, that can be robbed of their beauty by grey skies.

Reflecting water, then, is not only beautiful but provides an opportunity for the beauty of other things to shine. But it is not unique in this. A field of corn, a mountain glacier, a freshly mown lawn: these, too, may serve as a frame or backdrop for the beauty of things – poppies, pines, children playing with their pets – fully to strike us.

The beauty of reflections in water would certainly be distinctive if some remarks of the German philosopher Arthur Schopenhauer are well taken. Schopenhauer is known for a philosophy of 'pessimism' that generations of psychiatrists have regarded as symptomatic of his depressive and cantankerous personality. 'Pessimism', though, is the wrong word. Schopenhauer, for sure, took a bleak view of human existence: it is a 'mistake', it 'ought to disgust us', and ours is 'the worst of all possible worlds'. This is because, subject to a blind 'will', our lives are governed by cravings for sex, fame, wealth, power. Men and women veer between a state of frustrated desire and the tedium of temporary satiation. (One of the two busts in the philosopher's study was of the Buddha, from whom he inherits his diagnosis of human suffering.)

Schopenhauer thought that there could, however, be respite, indeed eventual salvation, from the governance of the will. One type of respite is found in the disinterested enjoyment of beauty. Despite or because of his own gloomy disposition, Schopenhauer took most pleasure in the brighter forms of beauty. He did not reciprocate Richard Wagner's admiration for his work, his favourite composer instead being the bubbly Rossini. In the visual world, crucially, the 'most pleasant and delightful' thing is light, especially 'the incredible beauty that we associate with the reflection of objects in water'. The 'most perfect and pure of our perceptions', Schopenhauer continues, comes from 'the impression by means of reflected light rays'.

Schopenhauer gives a reason for his judgement that reflections are supremely beautiful. In experiencing them we are entirely 'freed and delivered from all willing', hence our delight is 'pure' and 'without any excitement of the will'. There is no pleasure, he is suggesting, that is further removed from our everyday drives and self-interested concerns than the kind taken in the 'lightest, quickest and finest' of perceptions – those of reflections in water. (The other bust in Schopenhauer's study was of Immanuel Kant, from whom he takes over the idea that aesthetic pleasure in beauty is 'disinterested' - liberated from the practical, carnal and other interests that ordinarily determine our pleasures and pains.)

The pleasure I get looking down on the glistening sea off the cliffs of the garrigue is, as far as I can tell, truly disinterested. It is not dependent, certainly, on the satisfaction of self-centred desires like those for profit, fame, or sexual conquest. These seem to be well out of the picture. So, Schopenhauer is right to regard the pleasure taken in 'reflected light rays' as 'freed and delivered from all willing'.

The trouble is that the pleasure people find in looking at flowers in a meadow or listening to the song of blackbirds seems to be equally disinterested. Here, too, there is time-out or respite from a relentless routine of willing and desiring. Aficionados of flowers and bird song will regard Schopenhauer's judgement that reflections provide 'the most pleasant' of all experiences as special pleading.

Someone inclined to agree with Schopenhauer's judgement may suggest going back a few centuries to a thinker who also saw a close connection between beauty and light – St Thomas Aquinas. For Aquinas, as for Schopenhauer, pleasure in beauty is disinterested. Beauty, he asserted, is 'that which pleases on being seen' – that which gives pleasure in and through being perceived – irrespective of any further beneficial effect it may have. But there is a more telling similarity between the two philosophers.

Schopenhauer enjoyed many of the effects of light – the lustre on metal, for example, shining jewels, and the illumination of stained glass windows. In the late middle ages, stained glass was the quintessential art, one deemed essential to Gothic architecture by its greatest champion, Abbé Suger, who in the twelfth century refashioned the basilica of Saint-Denis in Paris. Suger was hardly less enthusiastic about the beauty of gems. It is hard to believe that Aquinas, a century later, was not inspired by stained glass and gems to include among his conditions of beauty that of *claritas* – variously translated as splendour, brilliance, shining and radiance.

A historian of the late middle ages notes the enjoyment of 'luminous brightness' and 'fondness for all that glitters' – jewels, sequins, polished helmets and breastplates, glass - characteristic of the age. But it would be wrong to think that Aquinas's understanding of beauty simply recorded the prevalent taste of the day. Abbé Suger had already described how, when experiencing the 'multicoloured loveliness' of gems, 'the mind rises to truth through that which is material and in seeing this light is resurrected from submersion' in mere matter.

Aquinas, a Dominican monk, is in no doubt as to the identity of this truth to which the mind rises. Just as a home is not beautiful if it is empty, so there is no beauty in a thing except by 'the indwelling of God'. For Aquinas, as for many earlier theologians, the sun and light are not mere metaphors for God and his 'Divine Goodness'. Sunlight is a 'power' or 'substance' through which, according to one of these writers, God effects 'the birth of material bodies and brings them to life ... and renews them'. It is through His gift of light that God dwells in the world He created.

This doctrine of beauty seems to tie the experience of beauty to a particular sort of religious conviction – to faith in the God of the Abrahamic religions. (An important school of Islamic theology – the transparently named Illuminationists - subscribed to the doctrine.) But it is possible to extract Aquinas's insight into beauty from any theological commitment.

You can find such a extraction in remarks made, eight centuries after Aquinas, by a young Irishman who had studied the saint's writings closely. In both *Portrait of the Artist as a Young Man* and the uncompleted novel *Stephen Hero*, James Joyce reflects on Aquinas's theory of beauty, especially the condition of *claritas*. During a walk, Stephen explains to a friend that, when looked at attentively, the clock on the Ballast Office in Westmoreland Street is not simply an item of 'Dublin's street furniture'. This is because it can be an 'epiphany', 'a sudden spiritual manifestation': it can emerge in its 'whatness' (*quidditas*), its essential being. This, explains Stephen, is what Aquinas had in mind by *claritas*. It is the real being of something manifesting itself, shining forth.

In Joyce's account there is no explicitly religious content to the experience of beauty. Indeed, the nature of the 'whatness' or truth of things that manifests itself as beauty is left open. When, at the end of their walk, Stephen looks up at the clock and confesses to his friend that 'it has not epiphanised yet', he's suggesting, perhaps, that he doesn't know what this truth is.

Like Stephen, let us for the time being leave matters there – with the thought that we experience beauty when we have the sense of things showing up as they truly are. If Stephen is right, then the reflection of light that Schopenhauer, Suger and Aquinas find supremely beautiful is an epiphany of how things are. How this might be so is a matter for later chapters.

There's another claim of Aquinas's about beauty that, stripped of the particular theological significance it had for him, is a more immediate matter. 'Beauty is shed on the moral virtues', he writes, 'in so far as they shine with the order of reason'.

This could be taken in various ways. For example, as meaning that charity, temperance and other rationally required human virtues are themselves beautiful. But that would raise the problem of why the word 'beautiful' is used here – a word most at home, surely, in the sensory realm of things that have colour, sound, smell or taste. This is something Plato recognised: it's why he began with the beauty of a boy's body before proceeding to speak of the beauty of more 'abstract' things.

So I'll take Aquinas to be voicing a thought already touched upon in Chapter 2 when discussing the intimate relationship recognized in ancient traditions between goodness and beauty. Beauty, according to this thought, is an *expression* of the good – in the first instance, in the form of the demeanour, movements, gestures and comportment of the virtuous person. George Eliot urged her readers to appreciate the beauty in a woman that lies in 'no secret of proportion' but in its expression of her 'deep human sympathy'. She would have welcomed her fellow novelist, Henry James's, judgement that a 'most powerful beauty' resided in George Eliot's own ill-proportioned face because of the character and charm that shone through it.

More will need to be said about this thought, especially when it is extended to the claim that it is not only the human body and face that take on beauty through expressing the good. Art works, gardens, buildings, animals, mountains and of course reflections of light in water may all – so the claim goes – be expressive of virtues and for this reason, as Aquinas put it, shine with beauty.

This chapter has been promissory. I have asked whether there is a distinctive beauty, one replete with significance, that belongs to sunlight on the sea or, more generally, to reflections of light in water. The answer has been that, if there is, this is because it is both an epiphany of the way reality is and an expression of the good. Absorbed in the loveliness of the sun playing on the sea, so the thought goes, a person is simultaneously glimpsing a vision of the way of things and being put in touch with goodness.

4 'IN PRAISE OF SHADOWS'

It's late morning. You've been walking on the shoreline alongside a glistening sea beneath a clear sky. Now you walk up the beach to your hotel, a building that's managed to preserve its late nineteenth-century elegance. You go into one of the hotel's sitting rooms where all is cool, dim and subdued - protected from the sun by blinds, its leather armchairs umber and wrinkled, its floor carpeted in a deep red, and with silverware that has taken on a dark, smoky patina. You find the room beautiful.

Or perhaps it is early evening and you have been watching a flaming column of brilliant reflections on the sea as the sun descends behind the hills surrounding the bay. Your gaze turns to an old reed hut further along the bay – a hut that you are now viewing in an autumn dusk. Here, too, you experience beauty.

These examples borrow from the words of two Japanese authors. The bayside hut glimpsed at twilight figures in a famous poem by the medieval poet, Fujiwara no Teika, while the smoky silverware is described in a celebrated essay of 1933 by the novelist, Junichirō Tanizaki. The title of this essay, *In Praise of Shadows*, is a convenient one for the present chapter.

It is from these authors that I borrow because the kind of taste that the examples illustrate is a characteristically Japanese one – a taste that has informed poems, gardens, paintings and music for at least a millennium. It is a taste for the smoky, the misty, the crepuscular, the shadowy, the weathered, the veiled and the murky – sometimes for several of these in combination, as when the poet Issa describes how 'the river's mist helps out the haze on a moonlit night'. Tanizaki exhorts us to appreciate not just the dark, smoky patina of antique silverware, but 'patterns of shadows', the 'mysterious gloom of a temple', the dull shine of a lacquer soup-bowl, the 'low, burnished radiance' of a Buddha's halo, even the 'ghostly beauty' he finds in the black-dyed teeth of traditional Japanese women. Many of the quiet, often colourless gardens made by Zen monks provide a fitting environment for the exercise of this taste, and the soundtrack of any film about it would surely be provided by the breathy, bending sounds of the shakuhachi, a Japanese bamboo flute.

It is important to distinguish two aspects or ingredients of the kind of taste or sensibility indicated by these examples, even if they often combine and merge.

First, it is a taste for the indistinct, for what is lacking in sharpness and clarity of form, for what is suggestive rather than 'in your face'. It is better, wrote Kamo no Chōmei, a Buddhist recluse and poet, around 1200, to 'gaze upon the autumn hills half-concealed by a curtain of mist' and to look at scarlet leaves when they are 'veiled', rather than 'spread out with dazzling clarity'.

The second aspect is appreciation of what is subdued – the 'immutable tranquility' of a shadowy alcove described by Tanizaki, for example, or the faded beauty of a reed hut or a frayed scroll. This may be the 'tranquil, austere beauty, the cool stark beauty' that is suggested by a word that has caught on among designers in the West – wabi, a term that originally referred to being poor or lacking in something.

Appreciation of the indistinct and the subdued is not, of course, confined to Japan. You don't have to be from Tokyo or Kyoto to experience the beauty of the worn armchairs in a darkened hotel room. And it was, after all, an English poet, John Keats, who praised the autumn mists and 'barréd clouds' that 'bloom the soft-dying day'. It was an Italian artist, Leonardo da Vinci, who championed the sfumato (smoky) style of painting in which shadows are to be 'left confused and blended', and as imprecise as they are in nature. And there are exponents of the tenor saxophone in jazz whose tone is no less breathy, fuzzy and sliding than that of shakuhachi players.

Still, it is in the Japanese love of the arts and of nature that appreciation of the indistinct and the subdued is most prominent. It may not be a sensibility that, as Tanizaki imagined, sets his country apart from Europe and North America: but it is nowhere as manifest – nowhere as fondly proclaimed – as in Japan. So my discussion will remain tied to Japanese aesthetic experience.

One reason Japanese writers pay so much attention to this taste is their conviction that it is meaningful. Experiencing the beauty of the indistinct and of the subdued is replete with significance. This significance, it emerges, is of the double kind identified in the previous chapter.

Just as the 'luminous brightness' of reflections was, for Aquinas, an epiphany of the way of things, so for many Japanese writers is the beauty of what is indistinct and without clear form. A shadowy alcove and a gold-flecked lacquer surface seen in semi-darkness are, for Tanizaki, suggestive of the 'mystery and depth' that belong to reality itself. For the Buddhist poets of Japan, mists, clouds, puffs of smoke and other phenomena that form and dissolve before our eyes manifest the essentially ephemeral, transient nature of everything there is.

And just as, for Schopenhauer, sparkling reflections on water symbolize a good to which we should aspire, so for Japanese authors do the subdued and the tranquil. Tanizaki maintains that appreciation of their beauty displays an admirable tendency to 'content ourselves with things as they are'. This tendency contrasts with what is implied by the Westerner's taste for the gleamingly bright – an obsession with progress and 'bettering his lot'. When Sōetsu Yanagi, a twentieth-century champion of traditional East Asian crafts, contrasts these crafts with 'the showy, gaudy, boastful and vulgar', he is using terms that belong to a moral, as much as to an aesthetic, lexicon. Or, better, they are terms that serve to blur any sharp distinction between the two. Modesty and restraint are virtues, ingredients in the good life: crafts and arts that display them, and eschew the showy and boastful, can be expressive, therefore, of the good.

Is there a problem in any of this for the argument of the present book? Its theme is the significance of the beauty we experience in sunlight reflected on the surface of the sea, and in related phenomena. The main proposal of the book is that this beauty is an intimation of both the true and the good: it is an epiphany of the way of things, and an expression of what we should aspire to be.

What, then, of the very different beauty – of the shadowy and the subdued – encountered in this chapter. Can this be any less significant? And if it isn't, won't it be an intimation of truths and virtues at odds with whatever is intimated by the beauty of sun and sea? Won't the characteristic Japanese taste in beauty point to conceptions of reality and the good that are inconsistent with those found further to the West?

But there is no problem here. Contrasting tastes, and what they show, need not be 'at odds', and difference – even a very striking one – is not the same as inconsistency. There are a couple of things, moreover, to bear in mind before rushing into talk of tensions, conflicts or contradictions.

First, we should remember that beauty is often found in places and in works of art that combine the shadowy and the brightly shining. A main motif in the works of the nineteenth-century painter Samuel Palmer – for example, his watercolour of a garden in Shoreham - is the effect of sunshine penetrating a canopy of trees, to produce what John Milton called a 'chequer'd shade'. Think, too, of the technique used so effectively by Caravaggio and others to create a play between light and dark, *chiaroscuro*. Some of Matisse's most memorable paintings are ones in which the viewer is looking out onto a bright sky or sea through the window of a darkened room. In all these cases, the shadowy and bright complement and enhance one another.

Second, nearly all of us are able to enjoy both the sparkling and the subdued. I began the chapter with examples of people who move easily from the beauty of a radiant sea to that of a shaded hotel lounge or of a bayside hut at dusk. The Japanese, of course, are no different. Mount Fuji, writes the poet Tesshū, is 'fine against a brilliant sky, fine when wrapped in clouds'. A Shinto tradition of admiring 'cherry blossoms in the morning sun' and of appreciating 'clarity and brightness' co-exists, as Japan's best-known literary critic reminds us, with a Zen appreciation of 'tranquil, austere beauty'. More than mere co-existence, in fact, this is once more a matter of mutual enhancement. The cherry blossoms in the sun look all the better when seen as you emerge from a shaded and walled garden of dark moss and grey rocks.

Instead of speaking of conflict and tension, we should accept that beauty is plural – 'multi-formed and multi-coloured', as Charles Baudelaire put it. The thought to explore is that different forms or 'colours' of beauty signify different aspects of the true and the good. Virtue, too, is plural: there are many virtues and, while it may require intelligence and effort, it is possible to combine them within one's life. A natural proposal to make is that a mode of beauty – that of the subdued and indistinct, for example – expresses only some virtues, such as humility and restraint, while another mode expresses other virtues.

A further proposal to consider is that reality, while not plural, has several aspects to it, and that different kinds of beauty intimate different aspects. If Aquinas is right, radiant beauty manifests the 'indwelling of God' in the world. If Tanizaki is right, the darker beauty of a shadowy alcove intimates a more recessive 'depth and mystery'. They could both be right.

It could be, too, that – just as different forms of beauty may enhance one another – the various dimensions of the true and the good that beauty signifies are mutually dependent. It would be rather satisfying to find that the famous symbol of yin-and-yang is also an apt symbol for the relationship between different virtues or different aspects of the true. 'Yin' and 'yang' originally referred to the sunny and the shaded sides respectively of a mountain. There cannot, of course, be one without the other, and nor in Chinese cosmology could there be the male without the female, or the hot without the cold – to mention just two of mutually dependent 'contraries' that the terms came to denote. The symbol of yin-and-yang is a circle evenly divided into white and black parts, with a small white circle in the black half and a small black one in the white half. The symbol is intended to convey that not only are yin and yang fused together, but that each implicitly contains the other.

Perhaps, then, the beauties of brightness and shadow require one another, and in doing so are expressions of the interdependence of aspects of the good and of the true. Perhaps ... These are, for the moment, only thoughts to explore as we go along. While the emphasis of the following chapters is on, as it were, the yang side – on the beauty and significance of reflections of sunlight on water – the yin side will not be ignored. Where it's appropriate, we'll adjust our vision and focus on the shadowy and subdued.

5 EXPRESSION

We postponed explanation of what reflections in water might express in order to take note of a kind of beauty - the shadowy, the indistinct, the matt - that may be no less expressive. And we need another delay, this time to consider the idea of expression. Expression is the crucial connection between beauty and goodness. Sceptics brought up in a modern culture that dissociates beauty and the good need to be persuaded of the existence of this connection.

A Sri Lankan teacher of Buddhist meditation remarked that the very point of 'getting up in the morning' is to 'awaken our mind' to natural beauty, to the trees, plants and birds in the surrounding jungle. Historically, though, Buddhists have been suspicious of physical beauty, especially that of the human body - above all, the female one. A woman who displays 'the sign of the beautiful', according to one of the Buddha's sermons, is 'the nutriment for sensual desire' and therefore, as a Commentary explains, for 'greed, hate and delusion'. So important is it to be weaned away from this desire that people are encouraged to contemplate leprous limbs and rotting corpses, which will rid them of any illusions about the beauty of the human body.

The ancient Buddhist literature, however, adopted a very different and positive attitude to 'beautiful mental factors' and 'beautiful consciousness'. These should be cultivated, not avoided. Modern Buddhist writers on beauty follow suit, emphasizing that the beauty that concerns them is 'inner beauty', or 'the beauty of inner states of mind', of 'inner reality'.

It is not necessary, of course, to be a Buddhist to speak of inner beauty. Most of us know at least one or two people we are ready to describe as beautiful persons, as having beautiful minds, or even possessing a moral beauty. Descriptions like these suggest a more direct connection between beauty and good than that of expression. Virtue and goodness, it appears, don't have to be expressed in the form of beauty since they themselves can *be* beautiful. But appearances are deceptive, and there is a problem with taking this way of speaking about beauty and the good at face value.

Plato, we saw in Chapter 3, was right to think there is an ascent to the idea of the beauty of knowledge and of virtue from the experience of sensory beauty – the body of the boy in the gymnasium, in his example. What Plato understood is that it is in the realm of the sensory – the visible, tangible, the perceivable – that beauty has its original home. Beauty, to recall Aquinas's gloss, is what pleases or draws us simply through being seen or otherwise sensed.

It's not a mistake to speak of beautiful minds or inner beauty, but we should understand such talk as deriving from an earlier, and earthier, discourse of 'outer' beauty. Otherwise it's unclear why we don't speak, simply, of inner goodness, saintliness, or intelligence. What warrants bringing in the term 'beauty'?

Buddhists sometimes recognise the problem and try to address it. They argue, for instance, that there are analogies with outer beauty that justify talking of a monk's beautiful mind – ones of harmony and balance, say. But these analogies are strained. The monk's mind is not balanced in the sense that a beautiful temple is. Or they may suggest that there is a causal connection between inner and outer beauty. The Buddha told a woman that being reborn beautiful would be her karmic reward for living meritoriously in her current life. But, even disregarding quaint examples like this, the suggestion is implausible. It is hardly realistic to think that the good looks of Hollywood leading men or the lovely figures of top Parisian models are generally the results of leading impeccable lives.

Here is a better way to justify our talk of inner beauty, beautiful minds and the rest. Virtue or inner goodness is expressed in facial expressions, demeanour, gestures, and styles of behaviour that are, precisely because of this, experienced as beautiful. Recall how George Eliot and Henry James found beauty in a woman's face because it expressed her sympathetic or otherwise attractive personality. Then, by a familiar transfer, beauty is ascribed to what is expressed, not just to the visible expression of it.

I say 'familiar' because this sort of transfer occurs all the time with terms belonging to the vocabulary of psychology. There is anger in the man's face, gestures and behaviour: so we use the word 'angry' to refer as well to the mood that all this expresses. A person's cheerful conversation, smile, and way of dressing express a personality that we also go on to call cheerful. More generally, descriptions of the inner are grounded in the outer: they are guided by what we are able to see and otherwise perceive. Perhaps this was Ludwig Wittgenstein's point when he wrote that 'the human body is the best picture of the human soul'.

So, yes, the Buddhist monk may certainly possess inner beauty. But this will be because his holiness expresses itself in an outer beauty of movement, gesture and comportment. Some Buddhist texts acknowledge this point. The Buddha himself, according to eye-witness accounts, was a handsome man, very attractive to women: but the texts also make clear that it was his way of speaking, moving and conducting himself that made him a person of peerless beauty. And that's because it was a way powerfully expressive of a 'gentle disposition', inner calm and enlightened goodness.

Some monks in Sri Lanka, one scholar explains, aspire to 'go beautifully in order to attract the people's hearts'. Through their dignified gait, clean-shaven wholesomeness, or gentle speech they make themselves 'beautiful to the eye' – or to the ear, when reciting verses – in order make people 'feel longing' for the holy life. These monks understand how lay people will discern in their outer beauty an expression of their holiness.

But doesn't a problem remain here? I pointed out that someone's good looks or beautiful figure is hardly firm evidence for their moral character. So how can we be sure that someone's outer beauty is expressive of inner goodness? Maybe the person is a mean-hearted yet skilful actor able to appear compassionate and gentle while being anything but. Maybe someone else is genuinely compassionate and gentle, but unlucky as well: his face and voice make him look and sound cold and indifferent. The body may be the best picture of the soul, but its accuracy is not guaranteed in every case.

There's no real problem here, however. The examples simply show that expression is different from evidence. A slow movement from a Schubert piano sonata may be expressive of sadness even if the composer was cheerful when he composed it. The sadness of the music, therefore, is no guarantee of the sadness of its creator – or, one might add, of its performers and listeners. Likewise, a face may be expressive of kindness even when its owner is cruel. A kind face does not establish the kindness of the person.

We can, though, say this. *Typically* or *normally* a kind face is the face of a kind person. Typically or normally a cruel manner is the manner of a cruel person. It requires good acting, dissimulation or ill luck for the normal connection between inner and outer to break down.

So we can retain the thought that outer beauty is expressive of inner goodness or virtue. It's not a thought that is challenged by the breakdown, in atypical cases, of their correlation. A face or gesture, we can still say, will be beautiful when it expresses kindness, say, or humility – when, in effect, it is a kind or humble face.

Here's another worry readers may reasonably have. Granted that the human face or body is a picture of the human soul, how do get from this to the thought that things in nature, like the sun reflected in the sea, can be expressive of the good? The goodness we're talking about, after all, is goodness of the human person: and how can anything but an attribute of the human – a person's face, say – express this?

Well, if your best friend's face is a kind one so is the face in an accurate portrait of her. A face may be a kind one, too, in a picture that is not a portrait of any actual woman, but a product of the artist's imagination. So something other than a human being – in these cases, art works – can be expressive of a virtue, just as they can of sadness and other feelings. It's worth noting, too, that to be sad or kind the face in a painting or drawing need not seriously resemble real faces. Good cartoonists can suggest sadness or cheerfulness, kindness or cruelty, with just a few schematic strokes of the pen.

And when we turn to music, the very idea of resemblance to the human face is hard to make sense of. Yet a piece of music can be sad, angry, pompous, humble, gentle, violent ...., just as faces or gestures can. Sometimes, perhaps, there is some resemblance between the music and the noises that an angry, sad or whatever person is liable to make. But only in some cases, and even in these the resemblance is tenuous.

But in all these examples, you may say, we are still dealing with the human – albeit with the products of human creativity, like drawings and music, rather than with the human body. So doesn't the issue of extending this talk of expression to non-human natural things still remain?

In response, it's worth remarking that natural objects or phenomena are integral to many modern art works. *Objets trouvés* – lumps of driftwood, say - may be incorporated into a sculpture, just as the recorded sounds of birds or waterfalls are blended into a musical composition. The artist or composer is likely to regard these natural phenomena as crucial to the expressive power of the work. Interestingly for us, the cooperation of the sun may be integral to an art work. In several examples of Andy Goldsworthy's land art, 'the sun performs its silent labour' – melting structures of ice or snow, for instance, or producing effects like X-rays on a surface of rock or grass.

The worry may persist that, in these examples, it is still something human – the art works, the musical compositions – that are doing the expressing, even if the human intervention is fairly minimal. But when I listen to the cheerful bird song in a piece of music, or look at the poignant lumps of driftwood in an installation, I am not – not necessarily, anyway – focused on what the composer or artist was trying to create. It's the blackbird's notes themselves, or the gnarled, bleached wood itself, that are cheerful or poignant.

It would surely be strange, paradoxical even, if natural phenomena could only be expressive when represented by, or integrated into, art works. Certainly it is familiar in everyday conversation – and not just in lyric poetry - to describe these phenomena in terms drawn from the languages of emotion and character. Bird songs can be cheerful, sad, harsh and tender. And the sea, we already know, has many, many moods – gentle, cruel, sinister, placid, and so on.

The point applies, of course, to reflections in water. It is a perverse idea that reflections can only express anything when painted by Turner or translated into sounds by Debussy. When Monet painted the sun's effects on the surface of the sea at Le Havre or of his pond at Giverny, this was because these effects – these reflections – were already expressive for him. They didn't have to wait to be painted by him in order to be expressive. His paintings, Monet once remarked, aimed to be 'mirror[s] of water', but it was the surface of water itself – marvellously 'altering at every moment' – that conveyed so much to him that he felt compelled to depict it, over and over again.

So the sun's reflections in water can express, as can countless other natural phenomena, including those, like shadows, whose complex interplay with sunlight was discussed earlier. It's time, then, to ask what it is that they do express.

6 **HAPPINESS**

This and the following two chapters are invitations. Invitations to consult your experiences of the sun reflected by the sea and to share my sense of the human goods that this expresses. Perhaps you won't share this sense, in which case my construal of such experiences is more idiosyncratic, eccentric even, than I would hope. Let's see.

Here, then, is the question: what aspects of the good life are expressed by the play of sunlight on the surface of the sea? Put differently, to what virtues does it give symbolic expression?

It is helpful, here, to repeat my warning about the word 'virtue'. I am using it in the older sense of an excellence, power or disposition of character. This is what was meant by the ancient terms – the Greek *arête*, for example, or the Chinese *de* – that are conventionally translated as 'virtue'. So, the word should not be heard in a narrowly moral sense – as belonging to talk about justice, right, duty and principle. The virtues I shall soon be identifying do not figure in familiar lists of moral virtue – alongside honesty, say, or charity – that have been drawn up in Western philosophy and theology. Indeed, unless you bear in mind the older sense I intend, my reference to them as virtues will sound odd. If it makes you feel more comfortable, visualize the word in scare quotes.

Here are three virtues, I propose, that are expressed by sunlight on the surface of water: happiness, spontaneity, and convergence with nature. These three are not separate. Happiness spills over into spontaneity, and together they require – and foster – a sense of convergence or intimacy with the natural world. Nor are these three virtues independent of understanding and truth. As the ancients rightly perceived, virtues must, in order to be virtues, accord with the way of things – with the world when it is seen for what it is. To have 'profound' *de*, the Daoists insisted, a person must discern the *dao*, the Way. The other ancient traditions contained a similar message.

In this chapter, the topic is happiness. In those that follow, I turn to spontaneity and convergence with nature.

Happiness has become fashionable, the subject of a whole branch of academic study, called 'positive' psychology. Angst, depression, and despair – the standard fare of so much twentieth-century psychology – have given way to a focus on the brighter side of emotional life. Happiness is now subjected, predictably, to a battery of scientific tests, from brain scans to psychometric techniques, that the attention of scientific psychology brings in its train. I have little to say about the science of happiness, primarily because the types of happiness it examines have little relevance to the kind that could be regarded as a virtue. I'm not especially interested, for example, when I read that somebody – a Buddhist monk, it seems – is the happiest man in the world on the grounds that brain tests show him to be enviably free from agitation and worry.

What I am interested in is how the sun on the sea may be expressive of happiness and how happiness can count as a virtue. These two topics are closely related: for to recognize what mode of happiness is expressed is already to glimpse how it may be a virtue.

In a book that pays homage to its subject, *Sunshine* – subtitled, *One Man's Search for Happiness* - Robert Mighall writes that sunshine is a 'prime metaphor for happiness'. He's right, and the metaphor fits comfortably into the large everyday rhetoric of happiness. Someone who is happy is said to feel bright, light-hearted or sparkling. Someone lucky enough to feel happy a lot of the time has a sunny disposition. By contrast, a person who is unhappy feels gloomy, and is in a dark or a black mood. Post-war depression in Europe came to an end, it's been said, in 1958 – with the appearance of the Italian song *Volare*. A lost dream or hope returns, so its lyrics explain, as the spirit soars up into the blue, ever happier as it flies towards the sun.

What everyday metaphors and popular songs convey is confirmed by many of the celebrants of the sun – artists, writers, composers – encountered in earlier chapters. 'The sun is glorious' here in Arles, wrote Vincent Van Gogh to his brother Theo in April 1889, so that people forget their troubles and 'brim over with high spirits'. Those who 'don't believe in the sun', he remarks, are 'the real infidels'. It was beneath the blue 'halcyon sky of Nice' that Nietzsche's spirits soared, while in one of D.H. Lawrence's poems the 'sun-women' tell 'how delicious it is to feel the sunshine upon one! And how delicious to open like a marigold'.

Does all of this amount to more than a reminder of the well-documented association between sunlight and good mood? Deprive people of sunlight and many of them will suffer from SAD, and the vast majority of men and women who respond to questionnaires about their meteorological preferences say they feel better when the sun is shining. But the entrenchment of sunshine as a prime metaphor for happiness is due, we'll see, to more than its familiar correlation with good mood.

Explicitly or implicitly, this prime metaphor often invokes the sea in conjunction with sunshine. It is specifically the sun shining on the sea that is a symbolic expression of happiness. On a morning in 1915, the Greek poet, C.P. Cavafy, stood looking – as he probably did most days of his adult life - towards the Mediterranean from the city where he lived, Alexandria. He recorded 'the morning sea's and cloudless sky's radiant hues; all beautiful and brightly lit'. Here, despite an effort just to see the scene for what it is, the poet is compelled to find 'ideal visions of sensual bliss'.

Sensual bliss, good moods, high spirits ... these and many other pleasant states may be signified by the sun and the sea. But they don't constitute happiness – not the happiness that people want their lives as a whole to enjoy, not the happiness that could count as a virtue. To get closer to the character of this kind of happiness, let's hear from two more celebrants of sun and sea.

In a letter from Venice, written on a warm day by the lagoon in the autumn of 1786, Goethe – who wondered how it is possible to live where the weather is always gloomy – exclaims 'Oh! If only I could send you a breath of this light way of being!'. Seventy years later, Matthew Arnold, a poet who did spend most of his life in a gloomy climate, wrote these lines, one suspects with some yearning :–

> Is it so small a thing
>
> To have enjoy'd the sun,
>
> To have lived light in the Spring'.

Happiness, for these poets, is a way of living or being – a 'light' way that the sun both facilitates and symbolizes. And this suggests a better way of understanding happiness, one that gets us away from a preoccupation with passing pleasures, blissful feelings, delicious sensations, thrills and titillations. Happiness – the kind we seek and hope to achieve – is more like a tone of one's life. Or better still, perhaps, a tone of the world that is present to us, the way it figures for our experience.

Ludwig Wittgenstein, in the so-called 'mystical' remarks at the end of his *Tractatus Logico-Philosophicus* – composed when he was serving in the Austrian army during the First World War – wrote that 'the world of the happy man is a different one from that of the unhappy man'. The world, he says, 'must, so to speak, wax and wane as a whole' for the happy and the unhappy man respectively. Like most commentators, I am not sure exactly what Wittgenstein had in mind, and my remarks are not an attempt to interpret his meaning. But the image of the happy person as a man or woman for whom the world as a whole 'waxes' is powerfully suggestive, and I want to identify what it might evoke.

The world of the person whose life is becoming happier – maybe after a period of illness or depression - indeed seems to grow, to become more expansive. It is not the hemmed in, closed off world of the invalid or of someone unable to see a way out of a narrow, tunnelled existence. The world of the happy person becomes more open, turning itself into an arena of possibilities for initiatives, projects, enjoyments and fresh commitments. To become open in this way, the world of the happy person must, so to speak, be a vista, something visible and surveyable: the possibilities that it enables, or indeed *is*, must be lit up like a clearing in a forest. Otherwise it cannot be experienced as the theatre of opportunities and initiatives that it needs to be in order to be open and expansive.

It must be a world, too, that quickens, that gives out an impression of energy and animation: a place that is not fixed and static, but one where there is movement and vigour. Otherwise it won't figure as an arena in which people's own returning energy will find a response and, as it were, be reflected back to them. And it must be experienced as a buoyant world, one in which the projects and commitments a person undertakes will be supported, kept afloat, and so have a good chance of success or consummation. A world that is experienced as buoyant is one in which a person is able to feel hope, and hope is a precondition of making the attempt to shape a life that will flourish.

If this is how the world of the happy man must be then it is not hard to see why the sun on the sea is an expression of the kind of happiness that he enjoys. Think of an expanse of sea on which the sun shines. It is lit up, an open vista without obvious limits or boundaries, charged with sparkling energy, its waves buoyantly dancing across the surface. This expanse of ocean, quickened by sunlight, is an analogue of the world as a whole as it figures for and presents itself to the happy person. What the sunlit sea literally is – bright, lit up, open, expansive, surveyable, energized, buoyant – the waxing world of the happy person is metaphorically. That's why the sun on the sea is such an apt symbolic expression of the happy person's world, of happiness itself. It provides us with an image, a prime metaphor, of how, if we are to be happy, the world needs to be present to us.

Sun on sea, I promised, would be expressive of virtue - but is happiness really a virtue? Not if it is equated with Cavafy's 'sensual bliss', or with good moods and relaxed contentment. There is no need to deny that these may be constituents of a good life. But you don't have to be a kill-joy puritan to think that sensual bliss fails to qualify as a virtue; nor do you have to dismiss benign moods and contentment as trivial matters to think that these also fail to qualify. The problem with all these constituents is that they might, all too easily, belong to a life that, as a whole, goes badly – the life, say, of an obsessive glutton or a glazed-eyed lotus-eater.

The happiness of which I spoke – that of the person for whom the world waxes – doesn't face this problem Still, isn't this kind of happiness at best the result or outcome of virtue, not a virtue itself? That I experience my world as I do is not something – is it? – to admire me for.

The point implied by these questions is half-right. It is true that, strictly speaking, it is not happiness that is a virtue, but the *cultivation* of happiness. And we need to be clear that the experience of the world as waxing requires cultivation. It is not due to luck or grace alone: people have to 'work at it'. Only for a person who *tries* to find scope for commitments and projects will the world open itself up as an arena in which it is possible to find them.

But it's wrong to speak of this cultivation of happiness as a mere means to some outcome – happiness itself. Integral to the experience of the happy person whose world waxes are precisely the initiatives, exercises of the imagination, and investments in a future full of hope that help this world to figure as a theatre of possibilities. Aristotle proposed that happiness is not the product of virtue, rather it is 'an activity of the soul in accordance with virtue'. 'Soul', to the modern ear, sounds too ethereal perhaps: but Aristotle's point is essentially the one I just made. The happy person is the one whose own activity has helped to shape a world that is - and is experienced as – an environment in which the person's life is able to flourish.

But suppose the world as it really is bears little resemblance to the one that waxes for the happy man or woman. Perhaps the way it figures for them is an illusion: the world is not, in truth, open, expansive, buoyant and surveyable. This possibility means that the status of happiness as virtue – or more exactly, of the cultivation of happiness – must be provisional. For a virtue, in order to be a virtue, must accord with the way of things. *De* must be in harmony with *dao*.

But just as attention to the expressive metaphor of the sun on the sea led us to the idea of a certain kind of happiness as a virtue, so eventually the same metaphor will evoke a certain conception of the way of things, of reality. The anticipation is that the world really is as it needs to be for the cultivation of happiness to qualify as an authentic virtue. And the same thing is anticipated in connection with the other two virtues I mentioned – spontaneity and convergence with nature. Let's now turn our attention to these.

7 SPONTANEITY

The cultivation of happiness, I've urged, is a virtue. It is a condition for the making of a good life. But it is not the only virtue and not the only condition. Unless balanced or tempered by other virtues, the style of life of the happy person could – for all I've said to the contrary – be too muscular and strident to be one that we should admire and emulate. The world must indeed be experienced as open and buoyant, as an invitation to initiative and imaginative projects, if it is to be the waxing world of the happy person. But left like that, the exemplar of the good life might be of a sort of 'existentialist hero', someone of iron-jawed, energetic and unbending commitment to projects that he has, with single-minded determination, chosen to complete.

More 'feminine', less muscular virtues should also be cultivated – ones that temper or soften the contours of the world as it may be present itself to the happy person. The first of these further virtues I call 'spontaneity'.

Spontaneity, on its everyday understanding, gets a mixed press. We like it when people make spontaneous gestures – hugging a lover, say, out of unforced affection, not out of duty. Spontaneous wit is more appealing than laboured humour. On the other hand, 'spontaneity' may also suggest caprice and indulgence in gratuitous acts that are performed for no reason at all. In the case of a joyful impulse to take off one's shoes and run along the beach, this may be something to admire or condone. But not when more deliberate and considered action is required. Most of us wouldn't want our dentists or taxi drivers, when doing their job, to act 'on the spur of the moment'. So it is spontaneity in a slightly different sense from the everyday one that I shall be talking about and inviting you to regard as a virtue.

Let's work our way towards identifying this virtue by reflecting on a central term in Daoist thinking, *ziran*, that is often translated as 'spontaneity' or 'naturalness'. And let's follow the lead of the Daoist texts and do this by reflecting first on the primary metaphor used to express this virtue - water.

Water plays a rich and varied range of symbolic roles in East Asian religious and philosophical traditions. It has an important place, for example, in several Shinto practices designed to cleanse people of spiritual impurities – the *misogi* ritual, for instance, in which white-clad participants stand beneath a sacred waterfall. Confucius is reported as declaring great admiration for water – sighing, on occasion, 'Water! Oh, water!' – and he certainly employed it as a metaphor for several of the lessons he taught. A river, he said, symbolizes life's ceaseless passing, and the behaviour of a man whose reputation is exaggerated is compared to running water that has no 'ample source'.

But it is above all in the texts of Daoism – which has been called 'the water-course way' – that the imagery of water is at its richest. The 'highest good is like water', announces the *Daodejing*, which then goes on to compare the *dao* itself to water. The Way, like water, 'flows everywhere ... All things rely on it for existence'. Just as water 'preserves and nourishes all things, but does not claim to be master over them', so it is with the *dao*. 'Cosmic' uses of the metaphor like this one will occupy us in later chapters, but for the present it is the employment of water metaphors to express aspects of the life and character of the sage – the exemplary person – that is relevant. The sage's humility, for instance, is represented by water's tendency to flow down to the lowest places. The benefits that his example brings to others is compared to the manner in which water helps plants to grow.

But it is water (whose nature is itself said to be 'female', 'maternal') as an expression of the 'feminine' virtue of *ziran*, spontaneity, that is the most conspicuous and developed metaphor in the texts.

Daoist authors refer to water in many of the forms in which it is encountered – turbid ponds, rolling rivers, sewage even. Not all of these are apt metaphors for spontaneity. An image that certainly is apt is the surface of a brightly lit, though not glaring, surface of a body of water that, while comparatively still, is both gently moving and slightly agitated. The authors of the classic texts lived far from the sea during a period, that of 'the Warring States', in which travel was difficult and dangerous. So it is more likely that rivers, rather than the sea, provided them with this image. But I like to think that, had they watched the tide quietly moving over a beach – with the sun and a soft breeze playing on the waves and foam – this would have become their preferred image and metaphor of spontaneity.

For here they would experience a scene of fluency and flow, and the supple merging and separation of waves and points of light – a scene in which nothing is rigid or mechanical. They would find it, too, a scene in which everything is responsive, quickly and effortlessly adjusting to its context. The incoming water parts and moves round the rocks that stand out to sea; the waves flatten and change to foam as they strike the sand; the surface of the sea, at once still and agile, reflects the sun, the rocks, and the boats that bob about. Nothing in the scene would strike the observer as contending or imposing itself: nothing, to recall the words of the *Daodejing*, would be making a claim to be the master of anything. Nothing, one might say, is commandeered into serving a goal that is being relentlessly pursued. Everything is experienced as natural: the unfolding of a process without purpose. Everything is *ziran*, spontaneous.

If water in the form or manifestation I've just described provides Daoists with an image of spontaneity, so does the figure of a person immersed in water – the swimmer. The *Zhuangzi* records an episode when some travellers, including Confucius, are impressed by the sight of an old man expertly and effortlessly swimming in water too turbulent even for fish and turtles. Confucius asks the man if he has a special technique. 'No', comes the reply, 'I grew up in what is natural to me ... I enter with the inflow, and emerge with the outflow. I just follow the Way of the water itself, and do not impose any way of my own upon it'.

Reflection on the images of water and swimming inspires among Daoists a conception of spontaneity that distinguishes the life of the sage, the exemplary person whose life goes well. This is not, as a great commentator on Chinese philosophy put it, 'a *wrong* kind of spontaneity, the surrender to the passions that distort awareness'. It is not, that is, spontaneity in the shape of caprice and impulse. Instead, it is the spontaneity of people who are mindful and alert to their world - and to themselves, too. They are people, therefore, who need to be calm, relaxed and responsive. 'The right kind' of spontaneity, the same author continues, is 'responsiveness in the impersonal calm when vision is most lucid'.

The responsive person is one who, as the texts tell us, does not 'force things', but instead 'follows along' with them. In this respect, he or she emulates gently flowing water and the effortless swimmer. Spontaneity is the tone of a life that is free from control by inflexible plans, rigid conventions and mechanical routines. Supple, uncontending, pliant, receptive, 'feminine' – it is a life aptly and beautifully expressed in metaphors of bright flowing water and the swimmer who 'just follows the Way of water'.

The question that was raised about happiness in the previous chapter – 'But is it a virtue?' – will also be asked about spontaneity. And it will invite similar replies. First, its status as a virtue is provisional. The final reason why human beings should live spontaneously or naturally is that, in the words of the *Daodejing*, the *dao* itself 'follows the way of spontaneity'. In emulating water, the sage is therefore emulating the way of things: this is why spontaneity is a virtue. Once again, then, we must await an account of what this way is, an account of the truth of the world, before concluding that there is an authentic virtue here.

But, second, and ahead of that conclusion, the spontaneous life is surely an intuitively appealing one. It is a life most of us would want to lead.

Who, after all, wants to be like a machine, trapped in an existence of unbending routine and rigid convention? According to the classic Daoist texts, it is when spontaneity is lost that human life atrophies and is experienced as empty. People then fill this vacuum with frenetic activity, the obsessive prescription of goals and objectives, and fanatical devotion to achieving these. 'The multitude must all have something to do', and everyone is 'scurrying around even when sitting still'. No longer capable of flexible responses to lucidly experienced situations, human beings concoct regulations, conventions, rituals and principles to govern what they can and cannot do, think and feel. Life becomes regimented.

Next, if it worries you that spontaneity may be, as in the case of Zhuangzi's swimmer, too much of a natural gift to be comfortably described as a virtue, then you can repeat the manoeuvre of the previous chapter. Strictly speaking, the virtue is not spontaneity itself, but the cultivation of spontaneity among those people – nearly all of us, surely – in whom it is not an innate endowment.

Finally, I began this chapter by worrying that the virtue of happiness might, standing by itself, be too muscular, too much the property of the macho existentialist hero who stamps his will on the world. 'Know the male but preserve the female', the *Daodejing* advises, and proceeds to praise the 'feminine' qualities of receptivity, sensitivity and stillness. But the reverse advice is also pertinent. Spontaneity, left by itself, is in danger of decaying into passivity, into a way of life that *only* responds, that is purely *re*active - like that of a jelly-fish. To avert this danger, spontaneity needs to be balanced with the happiness of someone for whom the world waxes as an arena in which to act. The natural responsiveness of the swimmer to the sea's currents and eddies is something to admire, but sometimes at least we want the swimmer to be going somewhere, to be in the water for some purpose.

It is this kind of balance between two virtues that Zhuangzi had in mind when he invoked the famous contrast between yin and yang. These, we already know, are interdependent and complementary powers – associated with the female and male respectively - that hold sway over things and ensure balance in nature. The true sage is a person who, like flowing water, combines stillness and motion. As Zhuangzi puts it, 'in stillness', the sage 'shares the power in yin, [and] in motion shares the surge of yang'. That's not a bad way of articulating the balance of two virtues – of happiness and spontaneity – that are harmonized in a human life that goes well. This is a balance that needs to be maintained when, as is about to happen, one further virtue is introduced into the conditions for a good life.

8 CONVERGENCE WITH NATURE

It's a cold early morning in late May, and I am sitting on a bench in my garden, my hands around a cup of coffee. Because of the long, exceptionally chilly winter the blossom on the apple and pear trees is still flowering. Indeed, some buds are still waiting to come out. The sun is shining on the blossom, as it is on the surface of the small pond between the fruit trees – a sun that has energized the sparrows, finches and starlings, and inspired them to sing out after weeks of greyness. The experience is one of beauty, of course, but more than this it is one of intimacy or convergence with nature. Maybe it's this that gives to the experience its beauty.

A sense of convergence with the natural world feels good. More than that, however, it is a feeling that it is good to have – one worth cultivating and nursing. There is surely something wrong with people who, in Woody Allen's phrase, feel 'at two with nature'. Few of us would want our friends or children to adopt the attitude expressed by the Austrian novelist, Thomas Bernhard: 'I hate [nature] … I love everything except nature because nature seems to me to be uncanny … I fear it and avoid it wherever I can … the countryside is always against me'.

What people call 'unity' or 'oneness' with nature is clearly something that many of them yearn for and actively seek when back-packing, bird-watching, or simply sitting in a garden on a May morning.

All of this suggests that convergence with nature – a sense of intimacy with the natural world – is a virtue. It promotes a flourishing, happy life. (The German philosopher Hegel gave the label 'unhappy consciousness' to the medieval Christian perception of the natural world as alien to the human soul.) I'm tempted, certainly, to see virtue in this morning's little experience of intimacy. Especially when I contrast it with the shooting of birds, whose banging sounds faintly reach me in the garden. This, I want to say, can't be the right way to live in relation to nature.

I expressed the worry in the previous chapter that the happiness I had spoken of earlier might, left untempered, be too muscular a virtue. This was one reason for introducing the balancing virtue of spontaneity. An allied worry is that the waxing world of the happy man might strike him as an open opportunity 'to command nature in action', as Sir Francis Bacon put it. Perhaps such a man would share the hope, voiced by a Marxist historian in words that give a new twist to the metaphor of a waxing world, that 'nature will become perfect wax in [man's] hands'. The present chapter aims to deter an understanding of happiness as something that could be derived from treating nature as so much raw material or equipment for human use.

The phrase 'convergence with nature' is a fairly bland one. Intentionally so, since the more familiar rhetoric of oneness or unity with nature encourages an unnecessarily paradoxical view. There is no need, in order to establish that there is an intimate relationship between human beings and the natural world, to subscribe to such exaggerated claims as 'the world is our body', 'all of nature, mountains and rivers, are seen as oneself', and that a person *is* the rainforest that he or she is trying to protect.

There is no need, in effect, to deny the many respects in which human beings are very different from any other beings in nature. No other being, for example, is capable of reflecting upon – and of writing or reading books on – the relationship between human beings and nature.

That said, it is certainly possible to exaggerate the divide between humanity and nature, to ignore ways in which there is a mutual dependence between them. And it is certainly possible, as we know from a long history of attempts to live in maximum isolation from natural environments, to ignore the value of a convergent engagement with these environments.

In the manner already familiar from earlier chapters, let's work towards a fuller understanding of convergence by exploring the experience of sunlight, sea and reflections.

According to John Ruskin, among the last words uttered by his idol, J.W.M.Turner, was 'The sun is God'. Even if Ruskin was mistaken about this – and also about Tuerner being 'a sun-worshipper of the old breed' – the sun, usually reflected in water, became an increasingly insistent presence in Turner's paintings, the late water colours of Venice, for example. 'Insistent' is too weak a term, perhaps, to describe the sun, bouncing off the sea in the harbour of Carthage, in his work, *Regulus*. Here the relentless light is seen almost as it must have been by the unfortunate Roman envoy, his eyelids cut off and forced by his captors to stare at the burning sun until he was blinded.

For Turner, the experience of sunlight reflected in water is a clue to the nature of experience in general, and one that gives the lie to a prevailing model of perception. According to this entrenched model, perception is a mental act of attention, on the part of a subject, to objects out there in the world. Turner, influenced by Goethe's theory of vision, thinks that this model ignores a double involvement of the body in perceptual experience. The sun is not an object of Regulus's attention: rather, it inscribes itself onto the Roman eyes and skin. When, less painfully and dramatically than Regulus, we look at bright reflections in water, the light is not an object of a detached, spectatorial gaze: rather the light reverberates with us, it transmits to us, and penetrates us. (The idea of penetration of the body by light is not entirely metaphorical. Dissections of the heads of ducks in the 1930s showed that light had penetrated their skulls to leave marks on their brains.)

At the same time, *what* we see is not an ingredient of reality that exists independently of our vision. What Regulus experiences – the glare, the movement of light, the fuzziness of the buildings and the people that line the harbour - is a function of his body, his lidless eyes and his pain as much as of the sun itself. As the author of a perceptive essay on Turner writes, 'The direct interface of sun and eye ... overturns a stable separation between subject and object, between interior sensation and exterior stimulus.' The distinction we are forced to make on the familiar model 'between the radiance emanating from the sun and the subjective luminous effects in the eye of the observer becomes meaningless for Turner'.

The lesson to learn is that there never is this 'stable separation': experience of reflected sunlight is just an especially vivid instance of the double involvement of the body in visual and other forms of perception. Cool mental acts of attention directed towards ready-made, clearly defined objects are abstractions from – interruptions in – the ordinary course of experience. This is a central contention, also inspired by a painter, of the French philosopher, Maurice Merleau-Ponty. What Paul Cézanne's paintings conveyed to him is that visual experience is a 'circuit', without any breaks in it, that links us to the world. That's why, he concludes, 'it is impossible to say that nature ends there and that man ... starts here'.

There, then, is one way that the experience of sunlight and sea softens the contrast between ourselves and nature. We relate to the world for the most part not as minds attending to things that stand over against us, but as bodily beings that are 'inscribed' by the world and in turn give contour and character to the world that is experienced. To appreciate this is to recognize a sense of convergence with the world.

This sense is amplified by a further way in which we are bodily related to our world. This is a way suggested by the now familiar figure of the swimmer – Zhuangzi's perhaps – who moves through the water relaxed, but alert and responsive. Or perhaps the swimmer is Roger Deakin's 'poet/swimmer' who 'immerses himself in the natural world' in a manner both 'active and passive'. In his bodily engagement with the world, the swimmer 'allows things to swim into his ken'. Deakin was an eloquent champion of 'wild' swimming – in ponds, moats, lakes - and, more generally, of coming to experience and understand the natural world through bodily participation in it. Our perception of our world is not, in its primary form, that of detached spectators of the passing scene. Rather, it is that of purposive agents for whom things stand out and invite attention in relation to this physical engagement. Deakin's swimmer – like the surfer who is 'folded into the rhythms of the world' – exemplifies this larger truth in an especially salient way.

We are convergent with the world, then, through our bodies – bodies that are inscribed by things, that condition how things are experienced, and that by engaging with the world opens it up for us. It is a sense of this convergence that explains much of the pleasure that the presence of nature affords us. The appreciation of their environments by hikers, rock climbers, and swimmers and surfers, owes to their sense of intimacy or convergence with what surrounds them. It is a mode of appreciation that contrasts with the more spectatorial, detached mode of visitors to an art gallery. This is not to say that contemplation – stopping and staring - has no place in the appreciation of the natural world. Contemplating, I suppose, is what I was doing this morning, when looking out onto my garden with its fruit trees still in blossom. But, even then, there was the sense of belonging in a little environment: a breeze felt on the skin, the sunlit surface of the pond inscribed on my eyes, some faded flowers asking to be cut down, some small birds asking for the bird-bath to be filled.

Convergence with nature, then, has an affective dimension. To have a sense of convergence is not simply to recognize a philosophical truth about perception, but to feel an enjoyable intimacy with water, animals, flowers, sunlight, breezes and other ingredients of the natural world. This is what supports the judgement that convergence is a virtue, something we should cultivate if we are to live well.

To elaborate on this affective dimension, it is worth drawing on some remarks of Albert Camus's. French Algerian by birth, some of his finest essays, including his earliest collection in 1938, are lyrical evocations of the Mediterranean sun shining on the waters and beaches of Algiers and Tipaza. One essay describes young men stripping off by the sea at lunchtime, not because they are ideologically driven nudists, 'those Protestants of the flesh', but because they are 'simply comfortable in the sunlight'. They testify, in effect, to a unity with nature that philosophers have 'longed for' – a 'unity … expressed in terms of sun and sea'.

In another essay, written when Camus returned to Tipaza after 'days of exile, of desiccated life' spent in soulless cities, he speaks of 'coming alive again' in the 'homeland' – a place of sun, sea and warm beaches – that he needs. The calls of birds and the sighs of the sea revive in him 'a will to live without rejecting anything'. He writes of this refusal to reject anything – this intimacy with the natural world around him – as 'the virtue I honour most in the world'. For Camus, there is no better symbol of this virtue than the experience of the sun and the sea that, as he put it, gives expression to the unity people yearn for.

And a virtue it surely is – the virtue of convergence with nature. To cultivate it is to cultivate a sense of kinship that is a counter to, a cure for, a mood of desiccation and estrangement that soulless human surroundings easily induce. It is a virtue with an affinity to that of friendship. For friendship, as Aristotle showed, is also a virtue, a necessary condition of a flourishing, complete human life. It is this affinity that gives a serious, and poignant, edge to Axel Munthe's memory of his happiest years, 'when the world was young and the sun was my friend'. These were the years around the turn of the twentieth century when Munthe, a celebrated Swedish psychiatrist, was transforming, with devoted love and care, a ruined chapel on Capri into a fine villa overlooking the Gulf of Naples. In the 1920s the deteriorating condition of his eyes made it impossible for him to look at the sun. His friend was lost to him; he returned to 'the gothic north', and his life was diminished.

But friendships, someone will point out, may be based on illusion: people may be blind to the nature of their relationship, to the truth about one another. Similarly, it will be suggested, a sense of convergence with nature may be misplaced. Perhaps those medieval Christians were right: perhaps we ought to surrender to an 'unhappy consciousness' of the absolute divide that exists between human souls and the material world in which, temporarily, they are lodged. Or perhaps Francis Bacon and the Soviet historian I quoted are right: nature is simply raw material at our disposal.

Well, what such worries invite is the warning that the status of convergence as a virtue – just like that of happiness and spontaneity – ultimately depends on its harmony with the truth of things. We must wait for an account of the relationship of human beings to the rest of reality before final pronouncement on the authenticity of these virtues. Goodness and truth remain to be calibrated.

Provisionally, though, the verdict is that in happiness, spontaneity and convergence we have located three main virtues, three conditions of leading a fulfilled, flourishing human life. Each of them is metaphorically expressed by the sun's reflection by the sea, and this is a reason why this play of light on water enchants people. The experience of sun and sea – the pleasure we take in it, the beauty we find in it – opens up and guides us through the terrain of the virtues.

The virtues I have located are not, of course, the only ones. We should be alert to those, in particular, expressed by phenomena very different from those of the bright, sparkling effects on sunlight on the sea. Before considering these effects as an epiphany of the way of things, we'll first revisit some of those more subdued experiences that were described in Chapter 4.

9 HUMILITY

In 1324, at the age of about forty, a courtier at the imperial palace in Kyoto gave up his position, perhaps as a result of an unrequited love for a girl. He was ordained a Buddhist monk, adopted the name Kenkō, and went on to write a series of notes – when he had 'nothing better to do' – that form one of the most influential of all Japanese works, *Essays in Idleness*. More than any other single work, the *Essays* helped to shape the characteristically Japanese appreciation of beauty discussed in Chapter 4. With elegance and humour, Kenkō invites his readers to acknowledge and admire the beauty of what is indistinct, tranquil, subdued, ephemeral, worn or weathered. The beauty of a frayed scroll, for example, or of the moon viewed through a film of cloud, or of an unassuming garden where plants 'grow of their own accord'. Anticipating Tanizaki's 'praise of shadows', he expresses pity for the 'man who says that night dims the beauty of things'.

The man in question, quite possibly, is the one Kenkō admonishes for having a sense of 'superiority to others', for his dangerous 'pride', and for boasting of his 'talents' and 'expertise'. Kenkō's *Essays* are important, not just for the aesthetic sensibility they encourage, but for the connection they make between this sensibility and virtue. The unassuming garden, he thinks, is expressive of the unassuming, unpretentious personality that a human being ought to cultivate.

Kenkō was giving an early voice to a conviction that came to pervade the writings of Japanese poets, critics, artists and priests. It is the conviction, in the words of a contemporary Japanese-American writer, that 'moral and spiritual discipline is inseparable from engaging in aesthetic experience'. One eloquent voice attesting to this view belonged to a man we encountered earlier – the Zen Buddhist author,

Sōetsu Yanagi, who was also a potter, museum director and advocate of traditional crafts. In the spirit of Kenkō, he writes that 'to realize beauty and to practise [spiritual] belief are one and the same', since beauty of a simple, subdued kind is inaccessible to 'the self-conceited, the haughty … the affected'.

It's clear, then, which variety of goodness that – for Yanagi as for Kenkō - subdued beauty expresses. It is the virtue of humility, of the quality signally missing among the conceited, the boastful, and those with a misplaced sense of superiority and pride. The promise made in Chapter 4 was that, having examined the virtues expressed by sunlight on the sea, I would return to the expressive power of shadowy, subdued and indistinct beauty. It is, I propose, the goodness of humility that is especially well expressed by things and practices that have this beauty.

I speak of *the* virtue of humility, but it would be more accurate to speak of a number of virtues that cluster around the idea of humility. For, humility is a complex, many-sided notion. Understood in one way, it is not a virtue at all. No one wants to be humble in the hat-doffing, obsequious manner of Uriah Heep. Construed, however, as a healthy recognition of the limits to one's knowledge, it is surely a virtue – an 'epistemic' one, as philosophers call it, essential to disciplined, rational enquiry. And when it is understood, as by Iris Murdoch, not as 'a habit of self-effacement', but as a 'selfless respect for reality' undistorted by self-important ambition and self-serving prejudice, it is a form of goodness.

But let's be guided in the task of identifying the various aspects of humility – the several virtues belonging to the cluster – by reflecting on the expressive power of the beauty of the subdued. Guidance, after all, is the job of a good metaphor.

To understand how sensitivity to certain forms of beauty combines with an emphasis on humility, it's essential to bring out a feature of Japanese and other East Asian cultures that I have not yet mentioned. It is no accident that many of the examples of subdued beauty I have cited are of things or places that have a use – gardens, bowls, huts, scrolls, alcoves, silverware, and so on. These are things and places that, in the first instance at least, are not stared at and contemplated, but encountered and appreciated in and through everyday practices, such as gardening, eating and writing.

Nor, in East Asian cultures, do we find a sharp distinction drawn between these everyday practices and 'the arts'. The Japanese term *dō*, deriving from the Chinese *dao*, refers to a range of 'ways': these include the martial skills of *judō* and *aikidō*, *chadō* (the way of tea), *shodō*, (calligraphy, the way of writing), *kadō* (the way of flowers), and *kodō* (the way of incense). Crucially, each of these 'ways', as well as ones we in the West more readily call 'arts', such as painting, are regarded as 'practices of self-cultivation', paths of self-realization.

This has an interesting implication for how and why things and places are admired for their beauty. They are appreciated not as isolated objects of contemplation, but in relation to the people who make or engage with them in practices of self-cultivation. To admire a garden is, in part, to admire the gardener – less for his or her skill than for the spirit in which it the garden is made and tended, and the cogency and clarity of the purpose for which it was designed. The American pupil of a Japanese artist writes that the beauty of the master's calligraphy arises from 'the well of kindness', the compassion, it expresses. No final distinction can be made between admiration for the work and esteem for the man, for the work had become 'an expression' of the 'way' of the master. He and 'his art had become one'.

In the East Asian imagination, then, not only is the beauty of things 'practical', in the sense of being tied to the place these things have in human practices or 'ways', but it at once owes to and reflects the goodness of the practitioners. To see how the virtue of humility in particular is expressed by the beauty of the subdued and restrained, let's look at one especially famous practice, the tea ceremony (*chanoyu*).

Many visitors to Japan enjoy, as part of their 'package', attendance at a tea ceremony. Not every ceremony these days is likely to be 'authentic', but in theory, at least, the ceremony continues a tradition that reached its consummate form in the late sixteenth century. The early practitioners of *chadō*, the way of tea, were Zen Buddhists who wanted to develop a ceremony that would, as the best-known of them, Sen no Rikyū, put it, be 'in accord with the Buddhist path'. One of 'the worst faults in the way of tea', declared an earlier tea master, is 'self-assertion'.

It's been said that that *chanoyu* is a form of 'moral geometry' that 'defines our sense of proportion to the universe'. There's no doubt that this sense of ourselves in relation to the universe, and indeed to one another, is intended to be modest, humble. Many ingredients in the tea ceremony are designed to promote a feeling of humility: for example, the 'crawling-in' door which guests must, bending downwards, pass through to enter the tea house. An effective means for levelling differences of class or rank. More relevant for us, however, are the stratagems of beauty that are employed to foster this sense of humility.

The kind of beauty involved is, of course, the subdued one discussed earlier – the beauty of what is *wabi* or *shibui*, terms that indicate what is restrained, tranquil, simple and austere. To begin with, the comportment of the tea master, as he welcomes the guests and serves them tea, should communicate what Yanagi calls 'beauty in action', a 'lived' beauty. He must move and speak with discretion, attentiveness, modesty, respectfulness, and grace. Next, the utensils that are employed in the ceremony – from the tea bowl to the vase with its single flower, from the kettle to the mat on which a guest kneels – are simple, ordinary, and often flawed in some way, slightly chipped perhaps. The aim is to discourage attachment to a hierarchical scale on which art-works (and their makers) are privileged over ordinary objects (and their makers). There is, writes Yanagi, a beauty that 'asks to be used', not just stared at. This is not some lower sort of beauty: on the contrary, 'real' beauty 'shines forth from the natural simplicity' of these 'humble household utensils'.

The celebration of the ordinary by the utensils and objects in the tea room is continued by the buildings – the tea house, the waiting room – and the garden in which these are set. 'Delight in the refined splendour of a dwelling', said Sen no Rikyū, is a 'worldly' taste that the way of tea discourages. For, it is a delight that betrays a hubristic unwillingness to be content with a dwelling that is enough for our needs – one that doesn't leak, provides shelter and a place in which to eat and drink tea. The world does not owe us anything: we have no claim on it. That people find beauty in simple, austere and 'imperfect' buildings, suggests Alain de Botton, is a sign that, in a spirit of Buddhist humility, they have overcome 'the failure to accept the inherently frustrating nature of existence'.

The utensils employed, the environment in which the ceremony takes place, even the making of the tea are intended, moreover, to evoke in the guests a sense of temporality and ephemerality. The bowls and tea-whisks show their age; the garden – if necessary, through sprinkling appropriate leaves on the moss – announces the season of the year; the steam whistling out of the kettle before evaporating provides an image of transience. For Sen no Rikyū, the ceremony conveys a sense of time's flow, of being present at an unrepeatable event. It is a sense that renders the experience more precious, more beautiful.

What has that to do with humility? The Buddhist answer is that the perception of universal transience must apply to people as well. It brings with it the recognition that you yourself are but a constantly changing process or stream of successive events – just one very small stream, moreover, that merges into a great river that is forever rolling on. To recognize this is to understand that self-assertion and self-importance, pride and a feeling of superiority, are misplaced. You are not the kind of being – nothing is – that can properly invite self-love.

Yanagi sometimes writes as if the beauty of the tea ceremony is the only type there is: *chanoyu* is 'not a kind of beauty, but the law of beauty'. Elsewhere he is more catholic: beauty of the *wabi* or *shibui* kind contrasts with, but does not exclude, the beauty of 'the lovely and the gay' – the beauty, perhaps, of sunlight on the sea. Certainly my own voice is a catholic one. There are different kinds of beauty, and each is expressive of the good. The kind focused on in this chapter, which indeed contrasts with the beauty of the sun's reflection in water, is that of the subdued, restrained, shadowy and austere. It is a beauty sought and experienced in the Japanese tea ceremony, and expressive of humility, the virtue of men and women who have respect for the ordinary, are without a sense of superiority, know the relative insignificance their own lives within the cosmic process, and do not imagine that the world owes them a favour.

How well does humility sit with the other virtues identified over the last few chapters? Let's picture a person possessed of humility - Kenkō, perhaps, or one of the many poet-hermit-monks who have graced the Buddhist literary tradition of Japan. Their lives will be simple, undramatic ones, led in quiet appreciation of the subdued, restrained beauty in praise of which many of them have written. Do these lives confirm the prediction - or hope - of Chapter 4? Are they lives in which humility is comfortably integrated with the other virtues? Or, is there instead a tension, an opposition, between the virtues expressed by different forms of beauty?

I see no tension between humility and the virtues identified in earlier chapters. Indeed, it is surely a close relative of two of these - spontaneity and convergence with the natural world. Essential to the virtue of spontaneity is responsiveness, a supple readiness to adjust or change tack that contrasts with the rigidity of a mind governed by convention or fixed purpose. The humble, modest enquirer's readiness to revise a belief is a special case of responsiveness, prompted by the recognition that unbending conviction may be a symptom of self-importance.

Next, it is no accident that poet-hermit practitioners of the humble life, such as the celebrated Zen Buddhist monk, Ryōkan, invariably come across as men sensitive to and close to their natural environments – to the seasons, to animals, trees and mountains. Not only does the humble person refuse to set himself above other beings in a hierarchy of worth, but he is conscious of being folded into a cosmic process in which all other beings are integrated. A sense of convergence with nature, then, is a cousin of humility.

Humility's credentials as a virtue will depend on the truth of certain perceptions of reality. We saw, for example, how entwined humility is with a conception of selfhood associated with, although not exclusive to, Buddhism. This point is one I made in connection with each of the virtues we have encountered. It is now time to turn to the question of the truth of things, and to ask what experiences of beauty may show about the nature of reality. Can beauty be an epiphany of the way of things as well as an expression of the good?

10 EPIPHANIES

According to the Gospel of St Matthew, three wise men from the East, having heard the prophecy that the Messiah would be born in Bethlehem, followed a star until it stopped over a building. 'Overwhelmed with joy', they entered the building and 'they saw the child with Mary his mother'.

This is the event referred to in Western Christianity as 'The Epiphany'. The word comes from a Greek term meaning to 'show forth' or 'become manifest'. What the Magi knew only through prophecy was now shown to them in the stable at Bethlehem.

As epiphanies of the divine go, the sight that greeted the wise men - a baby in a cradle in a stable – was not especially imposing. Compare it to the one described in the *Bhagavad Gita*. This famous Indian text records a conversation, during a pause in a battle, between the warrior Arjuna and his chariot-driver, who turns out to be the god Krishna in human form. Having discovered this, Arjuna asks to see Krishna's 'supreme form'. The god obliges, providing Arjuna with a 'divine eye' to behold his 'supreme power'. Thus equipped, the warrior experiences a brilliant vision of suns, jewels, weapons, gorgeous robes – 'the whole universe', in effect, 'in its multiplicity, gathered there as one in the body of the gods of gods'. Unsurprisingly, Arjuna is 'shaken to the core', for he has not only seen Krishna in his supreme form, but has been 'entered into' by the god.

An epiphany, in the modern sense, does not have to be a theophany, a manifestation of the divine. Recall from Chapter 3 the epiphanies of which James Joyce wrote. An epiphany, for him, is 'a sudden spiritual manifestation'. What becomes manifest, however, is not a divinity, but the 'whatness', the essence, of something – of the city of Dublin, say.

In what follows, I intend the term in a fairly loose and undogmatic way. I do not insist, certainly, on a theological sense. It is left open, for the time being, whether the experiences of sun and sea that I'll discuss have a specifically religious import. Nor, as I use the term, need an epiphany be dramatic and sudden, like Krishna's appearance before Arjuna. The experience may instead be quiet, abiding, steady.

I retain from the ancient notion of an epiphany the sense of a showing forth - a becoming manifest to experience - of what for the most part is hidden, occluded or recessive. I retain as well the sense that what is manifested is something that matters - a significant, perhaps fundamental aspect of reality. One speaks of epiphanies of divine splendour and spiritual force, but not of cabbage leaves and rubber-bands. An epiphany, I want to say, is something that is experienced by a person as a showing or bodying forth of an important dimension of the way of things. An epiphany brings a truth about the world into the sphere of vivid personal experience.

A few examples will help to clarify this idea of epiphany. The early Greek philosopher Heraclitus is best known for his remark that you can't step into the same river twice. It was not, however, flowing water but combustion that provided him with an epitome of universal movement and change. The world is 'an ever kindling fire', and everything in it 'an exchange for fire'. In watching the log fire in the hearth, we observe in miniature the essential process of reality: the flaring up of a log and its disintegration into ashes perfectly exemplify the process to which everything is subject. The fire, for Heraclitus, is an epiphany of the fundamental character of the universe, a cosmic metaphor.

A very different example can be found in the novel that established Jean-Paul Sartre's reputation as a writer, *Nausea*. The book's central figure, Roquentin, goes into a public garden as dusk falls. He looks at the base of a chestnut tree and is overcome by the uncanny feeling of 'nausea' to which he is often subject. But now for the first time he understands this feeling. Looking at the chestnut root, he sees it in its 'obscene nakedness', devoid of any connection to human measure and understanding, disjoined from the human purposes and concerns that normally shape our perceptions of things. The root – and the world it belongs to – is experienced by Roquentin as 'absurd' or 'superflous', just 'there'. The root, in effect, is an epiphany of 'existence as such', of being as it is, in total isolation from our dealings with things.

Gardens themselves can be epiphanies. Certain gardens exemplify in a salient way a general truth about the relationship between human culture and the natural world. This relationship is one of mutual dependence. Human creative activity is always constrained by a way of experiencing nature, and how people experience nature is in turn conditioned by their cultural inheritance. Not every garden is suited to inspire recognition of this. Not those highly formal gardens in which culture appears to have stamped itself upon nature: and not ones, like those designed by 'Capability' Brown, that look as if they have never been touched by human hands. But there are also gardens – from Suzhou to Highgrove, from Kyoto to Lake Maggiore - that wear on their sleeve the interplay of human design and natural process, of art and nature. To walk around such gardens in a responsive mood is to experience in a quiet way an epiphany of a deep aspect of our world.

Do epiphanies matter? Should we, like the Magi following their star, seek them out? The answer is that epiphanies play important, even indispensable roles in promoting our understanding of things.

Arjuna had no doubt been told about the glories of Krishna by priests and teachers long before his meeting with the chariot-driver who turned out to be the god. But it required the great epiphany described in the *Bhagavad Gita* for this hearsay knowledge to be transformed into a direct knowledge able to penetrate Arjuna's soul and 'shake him to the core'. Likewise, as someone educated in a French *lycée*, Roquentin would have heard a lot about philosophies of being, from Plato to Hegel. But it is the encounter with an epiphany – with the chestnut root – that induces in him a vivid and emotionally charged understanding of being in itself, in all its 'nakedness' and 'absurdity'. Again, the Buddhists among you will certainly be familiar, at some level, with the idea of universal transience: but it may need something like the eponymous, ever-changing Japanese garden described in Tan Twan Eng's *The Garden of Evening Mists*, to 'reach inside you … [and] make you appreciate the impermanence of everything in life'.

So an epiphany may convert cool, abstract understanding into the kind of knowledge William James called 'hot and alive'. But an epiphany may serve as well to open someone up to an understanding that has been repressed or occluded. In his great sonnet of 1806, 'The World Is Too Much With Us', William Wordsworth regrets our inability, in a world of frenzied 'getting and spending', to 'see in Nature' anything that relates to us, anything with the power to 'move' us. To overcome the tendencies in modern life that degrade our relationship with nature and put us 'out of tune' with it, 'glimpses' of nature as it truly is are needed. A glimpse, perhaps, like the experience of epiphany Wordsworth described eight years earlier in his 'Lines Written A Few Miles Above Tintern Abbey'. There, in the waters and landscape of the Wye Valley, the poet famously encountered 'a presence that disturbs me … a sense sublime of something far more deeply interfused … a motion and a spirit, that … rolls through all things'.

The author of the *Gita* had a fair crack at trying to describe 'the god of gods' whose epiphany astonished Arjuna. Roquentin and Wordsworth, by contrast, do not attempt to describe, in literal terms at least, what has become manifest to them. This is for the very good reason that description would be impossible. Confronted by the 'absurd' chestnut root, Roquentin realizes that 'words had disappeared', and Wordsworth's spirit that 'impels all objects of thoughts' is not itself an object of thought that can be articulated in literal language.

So, it's not simply that, as every news editor knows, an image is worth a thousand words. In the case of some epiphanies, what becomes manifest or shows forth cannot be described in a thousand, a million or any number of words. An ineffable presence to a person's experience may be the sole way for it to enter into the understanding.

A final role played by epiphanies is akin to the function of good metaphors – guidance. In earlier chapters, we saw how a metaphor, like the sparkling surface of the sea, that is expressive of a virtue – spontaneity, say – may enrich understanding of the virtue. Likewise, an epiphany of an aspect of reality may further the understanding of this aspect or suggest fresh ways of regarding it. In Tan Twan Eng's novel, referred to earlier, the narrator remarks on the obvious way that her garden 'borrows' the mountain scenery to enhance its visual effect. But she then wonders if the Japanese creator of the garden also intended to 'borrow' the mists that swirl before the mountains - and 'the wind, the clouds, the overarching light' as well, even perhaps 'heaven itself'. The narrator's question illustrates how attention to the garden as an epiphany of art's relationship to nature may extend our appreciation of their complex interdependence. The epiphany leads us from obvious to much less apparent ways in which a human creation is a response to the world of nature.

Epiphanies, then, may help an idea to become 'hot and alive' for us, render salient a feature of reality that has become occluded, provide a means of access to an ineffable dimension of the world, and guide our explorations of the way of things. These various roles are all played by the kind of epiphany that is the concern of this book. In the following chapters I argue that sunlight reflected on the surface of water may be experienced as an epiphany of deep aspects of reality. That they may is a reason why such experiences matter to people and why they are found so beautiful.

I am hardly the first writer to propose that reflections on water are an epiphany of dimensions of reality, and I want to draw upon texts that attest to this. In the next chapter, therefore, I'll rehearse some testimonies to the epiphanic role of reflections of light. This will help me, in Chapter 12, to articulate my own account of the aspects of the way of things that are intimated by experiences of the play of light on the surface of the sea.

Several of the features of reflections I'll be discussing are ones already familiar from earlier chapters, where the subject was the power of these features to express human virtues. There's no reason why a feature of sunlight playing on water – its quicksilver transience, say – shouldn't be both an expression and an epiphany, why it shouldn't be a metaphor of the good and of the true at the same time. Indeed, this is something we might expect, given the intimate relationship between goodness and truth that the ancients recognized. Given, in particular, that a virtue's very status as a virtue depends on its fit with the way of things. So, in my final chapter, I'll be drawing together what our experiences of light reflected on water show us about goodness and reality, and hence about the nature and direction of life itself.

11 ASPECTS OF THE WORLD

Among the many fine poets of Tang dynasty China, the best known, in the West at least, is Li Bai (or Li Po). This eighth century poet is also famous for his drinking. Legend has it that he drowned when trying to seize hold of the moon, whose reflection in the water he drunkenly mistook for the real thing. The legend recalls a famous Greek myth in which another man meets his end through mistaking a reflection for reality. The beautiful Narcissus was punished by a goddess for spurning the advances of the nymph, Echo. He is made to fall in love with his own reflection in a pool. Unable to obtain the object of his love, Narcissus dies of heartache.

In tales like these, an association is made between reflections in water and illusion. Whether as the result of wine or divine spell, someone is deluded into taking the unreal as real. This association is sometimes exploited in philosophical texts. At the end of the Mahayana Buddhist classic, the *Diamond Sutra*, reflections in water and related phenomena – dewdrops, bubbles, flashes of lightning – are the favoured examples given of 'illusion'.

Does this association with the illusory make it unpromising to regard reflections in water as an epiphany or metaphor of the way of things, of reality? How can they exemplify the real and the illusory at the same time? These questions betray misunderstanding, however. What Li Bai saw was not really the moon, but it was a real enough reflection of the moon in the water. Reflections are not themselves illusions, though of course someone may, like the drunken poet and Narcissus, be *under the illusion* that a reflection of something or someone is the actual thing or person. The reflected moon or face is not an illusion in the manner of the 'blue mice and pink elephants' that Jack London tells us he saw during an alcoholic delirium.

There is no reason, therefore, why reflections should not exemplify aspects of reality. Indeed, they may be especially apt for indicating precisely those aspects that people are liable to mistake for something else. This is one of the purposes, in fact, of the passage I cited from the *Diamond Sutra*. The world as we experience it – what Buddhists call 'conditioned existence', *samsara* – does not have the solidity and substantiality that we mistakenly suppose it has. Reflections, bubbles, and dewdrops – which don't even appear to have these features - are therefore suitable metaphors for how this empirical world actually is.

In what follows, I look at how, in various traditions, reflections in water have furnished epiphanies of some fundamental aspects of the world.

For the first of these aspects, let's stay with the *Diamond Sutra*. One purpose of the comparison between 'conditioned existence' and flashes of light, dewdrops and the like is to indicate the transient, ephemeral character of everything in the world. It is an illusion, Buddhists argue, to suppose that beneath the ever-changing parade of experiences, there exist abiding objects. Permanence is a quality we falsely impose on this flow of experiences. What more effective epiphany, then, of worldly transience than a sparkling sequence of momentary flickers of light on the surface of water?

For Buddhists – though not just for them - this same mobile, flickering and swirling vista is an epiphany of a related aspect of the world. This world, in the view of several Mahayana schools, is a 'quicksilver universe … wherein all is seen as a flow lacking hard edges'. If permanence is an illusion, so too is the division of the world into discrete 'hard edged' objects. The nineteenth-century British 'idealist' philosopher, F.H Bradley, whose thinking is often compared to Buddhism and Vedanta, agreed. Close attention to our experience, he writes, shows that each object 'slides beyond its[elf] … spreads beyond its that'. It is we, continues Bradley, who impose structure on experience, and the separated objects that we think we encounter are only our 'constructions'.

Buddhists unsurprisingly employ metaphors of light and water to capture the quicksilver character of the world. It is a 'luminous flow', a realm of 'radiance, luminosity' and reflections. Some of Bradley's descriptions of experiences that are truer to reality than our perception of hard edged objects sound like ones of impressionist paintings, in which colours and forms indeed 'slide' and 'spread beyond' themselves. Monet's painting of the port of Le Havre, perhaps. Or they might be descriptions of the shimmering and barely defined wavelets that gently undulate over the surface of the water that Monet depicts. Or perhaps descriptions of the Solent on a day when, a keen observer of these waters writes, 'unresolved shapes drift by [and] everything coalesces, caught in a dreamy, half-hallucinatory loop'.

From the idea that things 'slide' into one another and lack 'hard edges', it is no great distance to the thought that, in some sense, everything is 'one'. This thought is often referred to as 'holism'. To be interesting, holism must be more than the uncontroversial thought that, at some level, everything has some connection, however remote, to everything else. I'll leave the attempt to articulate an interesting and persuasive version of holism until the next chapter. For the moment, I want to draw attention to how the guiding metaphor of reflections has been used by people who are attracted to holism in some form.

A question that taxed nearly all ancient schools of thought was how the world could be a unitary whole, despite the multiplicity of things that we seem to encounter in ordinary experience. Well, in just the way, according to Plato's philosophical heir, Plotinus, that light from the sun, while being itself 'single', produces countless reflections. These may look to be independent, but are in fact united in their entire dependence on the sunlight. Likewise, seemingly independent objects in the world are only 'acts flowing from the One', 'the source of all things'. Similar imagery is employed by the revered ninth-century Hindu thinker, Shankara. What appear to be self-sufficient 'elements and souls' are 'mere reflections' of the one reality, Brahman, just as the lights on the water are reflections of the sun or moon.

The metaphor of light reflected in water had a further advantage for advocates of holism. It serves to exemplify, not just the dependence of all things on a unitary whole, but the interdependence of things – the impossibility of understanding any one of them in isolation from the rest. Not only is 'the whole moon and the entire sky ... reflected in dewdrops ... or drop[s] of water', remarks the Zen teacher Dōgen, but the drops reflect one another. I look at the waves made by the ferry I am aboard, and in each wave that rises and runs on the water, I see not only the reflection of the sun, but of the waves that travel with it. Here is an aquatic version of the famous simile of the jewel net of Indra that Chinese Buddhists of the Hua-Yen ('Flower Garland') school used to illustrate the holistic character of existence. Strung along the net, each jewel reflects not only its light source, but also every other jewel in the net. To look into one is to look into all, and there is unity in multiplicity.

In some versions of holism, beings like ourselves stand outside of the whole to which everything else belongs. We are souls or minds set apart from the world that is the object of our thoughts and perceptions. But in more full-blooded versions of holism, the world encompasses us too as inseparable components of the whole. We too are fully 'enfolded into the rhythms of the world'.

We've already encountered, in Chapter 8, metaphors of light and water to express the intimate relationship between the world and ourselves. We are not detached observers of sunlight but, as Turner put it, 'penetrated' by it, and there is no 'stable separation' to be made between our sensation of light and an 'exterior reality' that is experienced. The Daoist swimmer is not gazing at a world outside of him, but is immersed in the waves and reflections on the water through which he moves.

In the same chapter, I cited Maurice Merleau-Ponty's remark that 'it is impossible to say that nature ends there and that man ... starts here'. An important theme in his writings is the idea that our original way of experiencing the world – long before we made a sharp distinction between observing subjects and observed objects – is a kind of 'participation'. The primordial way of seeing is not to 'represent' objects in the interior of the mind, rather it is to be 'immersed in the visible by [the] body', or to be 'taken possession of' by colours and shapes. Such is the closeness of intercourse or 'coitus' with the world, in this original way of seeing, that things appear to look at us as much as we look at them. To 'see the world is also ... to feel oneself *seen*'.

The shimmering, sunlit surface of the sea is an epiphany of world experienced in this primordial manner. Merleau-Ponty speaks of the 'ebb and flow', the 'flowing movement' of colours, and 'the vibration of appearances' in which we are visually 'immersed'. Only later are objects able to take on definite contours and identities, to assume their place in a world that seems to stand outside of us. And what better illustration could there be of the sensation of being seen or communicated with by the world than seeing the lantern-like flickers of light that reach us from the surface of the water? The flickers are 'Zen telegrams from the unknown', or 'ineffable glances' from sun and stars.

The French philosopher, we noted, was an admirer of Paul Cézanne. The painter's ambition, according to Merleau-Ponty, was to depict the world at the point where things 'take on form' and 'order' before our eyes, without as yet having been regimented by intellectual 'ideas and sciences'. Put differently, Cézanne's ambition was to depict the emergence of a 'primordial world' of experience through 'spontaneous organization'.

Spontaneity was the topic of Chapter 7, but this was spontaneity considered as a human virtue - of the Daoist sage, for example. The point was made, though, that this was a virtue only because it was held to emulate the spontaneity of the cosmos, or of the *dao* itself. Human beings should indeed 'follow the way of the *dao*', and that's because, as the *Daodejing* explains, 'the *dao* follows the way of spontaneity'. As the same text also explains, the *dao* is the source of everything, but unlike the supreme powers and gods of many religions, it is not a process with an end or purpose, it is not governed by some internal logic, and it does not 'contend' with anything outside of itself (brute matter, rival powers and demons, or whatever), for nothing resists it. It should be thought of, rather, as a 'giving' and 'nurturing' – of the yin and yang rhythms of nature, of growth and change, and of the essences or characters of the 'myriad things' that make up the world in which we move.

The aquatic metaphors for expressing the spontaneous life that we encountered in Chapter 7 are equally suited as metaphors of the *dao* itself. The way of water is an epiphany of the Way. Or at any rate, the way of some of the forms that water takes is thus suited. These won't include raging mountain torrents or motionless, turbid ponds. For Daoists, there could surely be no better epiphany of the *dao*'s spontaneity than a sunlit sea as it gently flows towards the shore. There is no purpose to the ever-changing play of light on the waves, and the water has nothing to contend with as it quietly flows past whatever lies in its path. At the same time, it supports the boats that rhythmically rock on its surface, provides nutriment for shoals of small fish that swim in it, and effortlessly carries driftwood forward towards the beach.

The chapter began with the worry that reflections of light in water belong to the realm of illusion and can therefore be no indication of the truth of the world. The worry was misplaced, and we've seen how, in various traditions, reflections have served as epiphanies of deep aspects of reality. In Chinese Daoism, Japanese Buddhism, Greek metaphysics, Indian Vedanta, British idealism, and French phenomenology we find images of light's reflection in water employed to illuminate aspects of the way of things. These aspects have included the transience of worldly things, their unity, their inseparability from experience, and their membership in a spontaneous whole.

It remains to exploit and combine the wisdom of these traditions. The task is to draw these deep aspects of the world together into an integrated vision of reality as a whole. It is the task, as well, to appreciate how the play of the sun on the sea is an epiphany of this

12 WORLD, EXPERIENCE, MYSTERY

These days I listen quite often to pieces by Claude Debussy and a Japanese composer, who died in 1996, Toru Takemitsu. Takemitsu admired his French predecessor who, a century earlier, had in turn been intrigued by Asian music. There is an affinity between their works, not least in the number of them that describe or evoke water. Gardens in the rain, mists, goldfish, reflections in water, sailing boats, and of course the sea (*La Mer*) are among Debussy's subjects. Takemitsu's titles include 'Riverrun', 'Rain Coming', and 'Rain Spell', and a work whose subtitle is a line from Emily Dickinson, 'Say sea, take me!', and which liberally quotes from Debussy's masterpiece.

The affinity isn't just in the titles. The deeper, yet very audible, resemblance is in a cluster of qualities that the aquatic subjects of the works seem to demand. These are the very qualities that were identified in previous chapter – aspects of the world that, according to various traditions, are suggested by light reflected on water. The music of Debussy and Takemitsu is another epiphany, in a different medium, of these aspects of reality.

What shows up with great clarity in these musical works is the intimacy of these aspects with one another. Here we have works of art, integrated wholes within which the composers combine qualities that invite one another. In the pieces I mentioned, the music gently flows and its lines are sinuous, sounds merge into those that follow, and the sense they convey is of a direction that is unfixed, spontaneous.

These musical works confirm what was already becoming apparent in the previous chapter. Aspects like ephemerality, soft-edgedness, and spontaneity 'go together'. It is no accident that a work – a Debussy

Prelude, a Turner canvas, a *haiku* by Bashō – that seeks to evoke one of these aspects is apt to evoke the others too. No accident, either, that the play of the sun on the sea is an epiphany not of isolated aspects of reality, but an epiphany of a world as an integrated whole.

What, then, is the vision of the world as a whole that is prompted by the epiphanies of which I've been speaking?

It is a vision very different from the versions of the world provided by the natural sciences and in everyday, commonsense accounts. These are indeed no more than 'versions' – useful enough for certain purposes and in certain contexts. But they are of the wrong kind to qualify as descriptions of the world prior to its subjection to human purposes and to schemes of thought obedient to these purposes. The truths of science and commonsense, as William James put it, are 'man-made products', 'carved out [of] everything ... to suit our human purposes'.

This is fairly obvious in the case of everyday accounts that describe a world of objects - hammers, trees, earrings, diamonds – that only figure for us, only get 'carved out', in virtue of their place within such human practices as carpentry and bodily adornment. But it is true, as well, of scientific descriptions, remote as these may at first seem from practical concerns. Nothing is allowed into these descriptions that isn't relevant to the eminently pragmatic task that first inspired and still sustains the scientific enterprise. This is the job of quantifying the world in order to enable the reliable prediction and potential control of events. Aesthetic terms like 'dainty', emotional ones like 'sad', and sensory ones like 'red' and 'sweet' are not admitted into the scientific vocabulary precisely because they are not geared to the tasks of prediction and control. Science comes too late, as it were, to be an account of a world that has not yet been regimented and carved up in response to human need and ambition. Like the commonsense versions on which it builds, it cannot provide an account of a 'primordial' world – of what Daoists call 'the uncarved block', and others have less poetically labelled 'The Absolute'.

The uncarved, primordial world, I want to say, is a perspectival whole of experience. This, in four words, registers a general, and compelling, vision of the world. The four-world formula is, however, hardly transparent: it needs unpacking, elaborating.

First, the world is a world of experience. 'There's but one Reality', proclaimed a philosopher we encountered earlier, F.H. Bradley, and 'its being consists in experience'. The point is not that the world is somehow 'inside', not 'outside', the mind. Rather, it's that any world we can think about and describe is not independent of how it is experienced. It is not some reality – some 'true world', as Nietzsche ironically dubbed it – that is set over against the ways in which it figures and shows up for experience.

Second, notice the plural in the last sentence – ways, not way. There is no single general way in which the world is experienced – not even a way shared by all human beings, let alone by all sentient beings. We might, with Nietzsche, usefully speak of ways of experiencing as 'perspectives' – ones between which it is invidious to choose. Only an 'arrogant and mendacious pride' could be responsible for people ruling out all but their own perspective – a pride, adds Nietzsche, as little justified as that of a mosquito who took its way of experiencing the world as the only true one.

Perhaps it's needlessly paradoxical to conclude that there's not one world, but as many worlds as there are perspectives on it. But this way of putting things is useful if it reminds us that, beyond the different perspectives, there is no determinate, structured world for any of them to be matched up with. And useful, too, if it indicates that a perspective is not a collection of atomic experiences but a whole, integrated way of experiencing. If I move to the left or the right of where I'm standing, everything in my visual field changes, however slightly. My visual perspective, my viewpoint has altered as a whole, and each element in my visual field is therefore modified. Likewise, all of a creature's experiences depend upon their place within its general way of experiencing the world.

A world then is a whole of experience, an integrated perspective. This characterization of a world suggests some further aspects. Experiences of things - even of those, like trees or stones, that we take to be pretty stable – are constantly changing. The tree doesn't look the same as it did a few seconds ago, before the breeze disturbed its leaves; the colours presented by the stone alter as I walk around it. Philosophies, like Buddhism, that emphasize the transient, ephemeral nature of phenomena are in effect denying the existence of a stable, structured reality set apart from our ever shifting experiences.

Once the intellect has got to work and carved this primordial world into discrete objects and structured patterns, we can predict and explain the occurrence of this or that experience. But before this happens, the world is experienced as spontaneous. Phenomena arise, merge, come apart, disappear in a fluid whole that is yet to fall victim to the mechanical models that human beings will eventually construct in order to rein in the spontaneous movement of experience. This primordial world is not a chaos, not a *tohu-bohu*, of sensations: but it enjoys a supple freedom that the work of the intellect will one day constrain.

The world as a perspectival whole of experience turns out, then, to have just those deep aspects of reality that were suggested to the thinkers of various traditions by sunlight reflected on water. The phenomena that belong in this world are spontaneous, ephemeral, soft-edged, intimate with one another, and inseparable from the perspectives of the beings that experience them. The deep aspects that, in the preceding chapter, were considered one by one are now brought together in a single vision of the world.

Correspondingly, we can now go beyond noting how this or that particular feature of reflections in water is a metaphor for this or that aspect of the world. The total, integrated experience of the play of the sun on water is now an epiphany of the world as a whole. How the primordial world is shows up in this experience.

There's something else this epiphany is suited to evoke – a truth about the world that has not yet emerged in my discussion. This is the truth of its mystery.

Schopenhauer endorsed the idea that the world we experience is inseparable from experience: it is a world of phenomena or 'appearances'. But he goes on to say that, were there nothing but these 'appearances', the world would, unbearably, 'pass us by like an empty dream'. Schopenhauer admired the philosophical traditions of Asia, especially Vedanta and Buddhism, and the point he is making is inherited from these traditions. There would, according to the man most responsible for bringing Zen Buddhism to the attention of the West, D.T. Suzuki, be a 'primeval awfulness' in the thought that 'appearance' is all that there is. We need some more 'affirmative and soul supporting' truth.

It is impossible, these writers are in effect urging, to live without the conviction that there is a *source* of the world of experience, of the ways in which it figures for us and for other creatures. Nor is it simply that we *need* this conviction, in order to have some ground, some measure for our experiences and beliefs. Some people, if Suzuki is right, also have a real *sense* of this source. They are capable of a 'double exposure', whereby the world shows up for them in its everyday ordinariness, but at the same time as emergent from a source beyond it.

Two dimensions of this source should be emphasized, both of them encapsulated in the Zen master, Dōgen's, gloss on the Buddhist terms for the source of the world - 'suchness' and 'emptiness'. They name, he says, 'something ineffable coming like this …an advancing [of] all things'. First, then, the source of the world is ineffable: it cannot be described or thought, not in literal language at least. As the source of all experience, it is not itself among the items of possible experience that allow for articulation. Dōgen's view is endorsed in many of the traditions of which I have spoken. Famously, the opening chapter of the *Daodejing* tells us that the *dao* that can be spoken of cannot be 'the constant *dao*', and that the relationship between it and 'the myriad things' – the world, that is – is a 'deep enigma'.

The Daoist classics teach that there is an enigmatic 'unity' between the source - the *dao* – and the world. It is nothing separate from it, unlike the creator gods imagined in theistic religions. The *dao*, like Dōgen's 'suchness', is to be imagined, rather, as a mysterious arising of phenomena, a 'coming like this' or 'advancing' of things into those integrated realms of experience that we call worlds. Every experience presupposes this enigmatic process of arising: but equally, no sense can be made of the process – the source – except by reference to what arises or advances in and through it. It is this source towards which Wordsworth was gesturing in the lines quoted earlier. This is a source 'far more deeply interfused' with things than a divine creator could be, a source to be pictured, not as a first cause, but as a 'motion ... that rolls through all things'.

Poets and presenters of television Nature programmes speak of the mysteries of the oceans, of 'the deep', to the point of cliché. They have in mind, usually, the weird and wonderful creatures that live out their existence in darkness at depths of several miles below the surface. The ocean is not a mystery, however, of the kind I discussed above – mystery in the sense of what is forever beyond the reach of description and understanding. The sea, nevertheless, provides an apt metaphor for the mystery of the source of the world. Mystery has its epiphany in light reflected on the surface of an ocean.

Earlier this year, I was looking at the glinting surface of the sound that separates North Skye from the west coast of mainland Scotland near to Gairloch. This surface might have looked like a two dimensional iridescent membrane that could be peeled off. But a surface is not like the ownerless smile of the Cheshire cat: it requires a third dimension, the body of which it is a surface. In the case of most bodies – rocks, logs, cats – only their surfaces are visible. Bodies of water, though, like lumps of glass, may be to a degree transparent. But when the surface of the sea shines, glints and glitters in the sun, the great mass of water beneath this surface is invisible. Its presence is sensed, not seen. It was, at any rate, on the day I looked out towards Skye. I was enjoying a 'double exposure': a lively experience of the reflected sunlight on the surface, coupled with an awareness of the measureless volume of water that supported this shimmering film. Like someone listening to a mercurial melody played on a flute while also being alert to the ground-bass that supports and secures it.

'Double exposure' was D.T. Suzuki's name for the experience of the world that people should cultivate – a combination of lucid awareness of the colours, forms and sounds that the world presents to us and an abiding sense of the mysterious source that comes to presence in them. The world is the visible face presented to us by an ineffable 'coming' or 'advancing' of the source, the well-spring, of worlds of experience. Here is a truth that finds its metaphor, its epiphany, in the lit up surface – the shining face - of the otherwise invisible sea beneath.

.

13 SUN AND MOON

There's a coda to the discussion of epiphany, one that's required in order to complete some unfinished business. In Chapter 4, 'In Praise of Shadows', the issue was raised whether the beauty people experience in the shadowy and subdued – in misty moonlight, say – is any less significant than the brighter beauty of a sunlit sea. We noted how in Japanese culture beauty of this kind is invested with a power to express and communicate the good and the true. The question of its power to express virtue was taken up in Chapter 9, 'Humility'. The answer was that the virtues expressed by the shadowy and subdued may be different from, but are not incompatible with, those, like happiness, that are intimated by the beauty of shining reflections on water. The question that remains, though, is about the power of epiphany, of manifesting the true. If a garden watched in gentle, misty moonlight evokes a vision of the way of things, is this a different vision from one inspired by the sunlit surface of the sea?

It's certainly seemed to some thinkers that the visions conjured by the contrasting kinds of beauty – by the sunlit and the moonlit – are not only different but at odds. The Japanese, writes D.T. Suzuki of his countrymen, are 'great lovers' of moonlight and 'semi-darkness', and this is related to their conception of how things are. Dusk, when the sun gives way to the moon, is the proper 'time of philosophy', says Erazim Kohák in his poetic work of phenomenology, *The Embers and the Stars*. This is because, in sunlight, things appear to have an 'insistent individuality', whereas, at dusk, they are experienced, more authentically, as 'fusing in an intimate unity'. This, in effect, was Suzuki's point too: the Japanese 'aversion to anything glaringly bright' is a suspicion of whatever is too 'distinctive in its individuality'. In the semi-darkness of soft moonlight, by contrast, the world appears as it really is, pervaded by a 'certain mystic obscurantism'.

A similar thought may explain Leonardo da Vinci's use of the *sfumato* technique. It's been suggested, at any rate, that underlying his taste for 'smoky shadows' was a belief that there are no fixed, independent objects, since ours is a 'world of process, flux and evanescence'.

But there's something strange going on here. The shadowy, subdued, dusky or moonlit is supposed, according to these authors, to evoke a world very different from the one intimated by a sunlit sea. But the aspects of the world that they draw attention to – the 'fusion' or unity of things, their evanescence and underlying mystery – are ones that, we saw, belong to a world made manifest in the play of sunlight on water.

There is, in fact, a confusion responsible for the conviction that the worlds respectively symbolized by the sunlit and the moonlit, by the glittering and the subdued, are contrasting worlds. The confusion is between brightness, on the one hand, and clarity or distinctness, on the other. This is a difference rightly noted by René Descartes. He seems to have disliked the effects of bright sunlight. This is because, he explains, the clarity and distinctness of things evaporate when they are looked at in the direction of the sun. Descartes compares a person whose eyes are dazzled by the sun with a lunatic who is unable rationally to distinguish among the objects and forms that make up the world.

Certainly forms do not stand out clearly and distinctly on the surface of a sea that reflects the sun. The water off the Florida Keys described in a poem by Elizabeth Bishop is a 'burning-glass turned to the sun', on which colours 'swarm', 'vibrate' and 'glitter rhymically to shock after shock of electricity'. Even on the less electric surface of the Solent, as we read earlier, 'unresolved shapes drift by [and] everything coalesces'.

So, yes, dusky, moonlit, *sfumato* scenes may well be an epiphany of the world, but this is the same world of 'fusion', transience, soft-edgedness, and mystery that we have already encountered – the same world that was evoked by the experience of the sun on the sea.

There are, to be sure, those – including Descartes – for whom it is the sight of things clearly and distinctly separated from one another that exemplifies an objective, rational vision of the world. But this is because, for all his 'modernism' and championship of the emerging natural sciences, Descartes had inherited a fundamental assumption of medieval Christian theology. God created an ordered world within which, from the very beginning, things have distinct and defining forms that correspond to 'divine ideas' in God's mind. When people see the world lucidly – and are not, like the lunatic, bedazzled – they perceive things in their God-given order and 'whatness' (*quidditas*). They do so by means of an 'inner light' that gives access to the 'divine ideas'. Medieval paintings convey this idea by representing a ray of light that connects the eyes of God to his saints.

Here, of course, is a conception of the world very different from the one that has its epiphany both in the glittering of sunlit seas and the smoky shadows of a moonlit garden.

Some people will wonder whether the vision of a primordial world isn't more effectively conveyed by experiences of the shadowy, subdued and moonlit than by those of sunlight on water. I've certainly had the occasional wobble when writing this book, asking myself if the emphasis should have been on the moon instead of the sun, on the gently glowing rather the brilliantly sparkling. But I think I've got the balance right, for there are aspects of the world of experience – its spontaneity, its quicksilver ephemerality – for which reflections of the sun on water provide the more telling metaphor.

But what about the world's mystery? Isn't experience of the sepulchral, of places in veiled moonlight, the more appropriate one for evoking a sense of this mystery? Story tellers and filmmakers who want to create a sense of mystery – a feeling that something strange and spooky is going on in the castle or the jungle – are unlikely to set the scene at high noon. Dusk is the time for the spooky, shadows the place for the unknown to lurk, and mists the atmosphere for alien noises to be heard.

But the sense of mystery that suspense stories and horror movies create through such means is not the sense that concerns us – not a sense of the mystery of the world as a whole. The world of experience is mysterious in virtue of having an ineffable well-spring: it is 'given' by a source that, not itself being an item in this world of experience, cannot be articulated. There's no reason for the idea of this source to call up images of the spooky, strange and unsettling. The mysterious source of thing invites, if anything, a mood of gratitude not fear, an embrace not a shudder.

Mystery in the relevant sense, then, isn't something that only the shadowy and subdued is able to convey. Moonlight and semi-darkness inspired in Suzuki a 'certain mystic obscurantism'. But it was Suzuki, too, from whom we borrowed the idea of a 'double exposure'. In the person who watches sunlight playing on the sea in a 'double' way – attending to the sparkling ripples, yet simultaneously cognizant of the depths on which these depend – the same sense of mystery is created.

People differ as to the images and metaphors that work most effectively for them. This is hardly surprising and no more disturbing in the field of experience that concerns us than in any other realm where human sensibility is engaged.

14 LIFE

The enquiry in this book was prompted by the question of why, as Norman Douglas put it, the sun's reflections on the surface of the sea follow you as inescapably as an insistent melody. More prosaically, why do so many people not merely enjoy but find significance in these reflections?

The staccato answer - that the experience is life-enhancing – only served to prompt questions about the sense in which 'life' is to be understood here. For such aficionados of the sun and sea as D.H. Lawrence and other vitalists, as I called them, the sense is a rather muscular one. The experience is a tonic that enhances vigour, vitality, eros and *élan*. Well, we may indeed want our lives to possess all of this, but it surely doesn't exhaust what we mean by the good life, the life we want to cultivate. It may turn out that these 'vital' qualities matter because of their place in a more fully imagined good or flourishing life.

For this fuller conception of the good life, I turned to ancient traditions in which it is understood in terms of beauty, goodness, and truth. A life goes well when it is led in appreciation of beauty and in consonance with what is good and true. The terms of this famous trinity were not, for the ancients, independent. Beauty, as Plato urged, is the attractive, magnetic face of the good, its 'symbol', as Immanuel Kant was to put it. But beauty is, at the same time, found in experiences that open us to the way of things, to the true. Beauty, wrote Martin Heidegger, 'brings about … the unveiling of being'. Goodness and truth cannot be kept apart either. My life is a virtuous one only when it is lived in the truth. My way must accord with *the* way of things. Conversely, I am lacking in authentic appreciation of the way of things unless this shows up in how I live – in my exercise of compassion, say, or humility.

A salient feature of the ancient literatures, we saw, was a rich use of imagery, metaphor, and other rhetorical means. The purpose was to attune people to, give them a feel for, and render vivid dimensions of the good life that are difficult, even impossible, to articulate in literal terms. No images and metaphors were more widely employed than those of water, light and reflection - often in combination. The ancient literatures encourage the prospect that experience of sunlight reflected by the surface of the sea will evoke the good and the true. This is, after all, an experience of beauty – of 'perfect' beauty, if Schopenhauer is right. Goodness and truth are made radiant in the beautiful, writes Heidegger, where they 'shine in the realm of the sensuous'. Beauty lets them 'scintillate'. Surely he was inspired to these metaphors by the sight of sunlight on water, on the lakes of the Black Forest valleys in which he liked to wander.

Encouraged by the ancient literatures and their imagery, we explored how sunlight on water gave expression to a number of virtues – those that I called happiness, spontaneity and convergence with nature. These may not figure on the usual lists of moral virtues, but they are virtues in the ancient sense of ingredients in a person's life that contribute towards the flourishing of this life as a whole. A further virtue – humility - also emerged when we considered the expressive power of the different kind of beauty that belongs to the shadowy and subdued. There is no reason, of course, why only one kind of beauty should be expressive of the good.

The identification of these virtues was, however, provisional. I followed the ancients, once more, in judging a life to be virtuous only when it conforms to the way of things. The good must pass the test of the true. We enquired, therefore, into the aspects of reality evoked by sunlight reflected on water. In this reflection, I argued, there is an epiphany, a manifestation, of the world as a perspectival whole of experience. This is a world inseparable from the ways in which it is experienced, a world of spontaneous process within which transient phenomena arise, merge and dissolve in an integrated whole. It is a world, too, that is experienced as emerging from a mysterious source, as an ineffable coming to presence for us of a world.

It might seem a remarkable stroke of luck that the same phenomenon, the play of sunlight on water, should be at once an expression of the good and an epiphany of the true. But it will only seem fortuitous to people who have lost the ancient perception of the unity of goodness and truth – a unity that, in earlier traditions, shows itself in the beauty of things. For to experience something as beautiful is to see it as the appearance of what is good and real. Beauty, as Stendhal remarked, is the promise of happiness – but only through promising as well an insight into a life that chimes with the way of things.

Here is how we might elaborate the connection between the good that sunlight on water expresses and the world that it symbolises. Someone who shares the vision of the world as a perspectival whole of experience will *want* to cultivate happiness, spontaneity, convergence with nature and humility. For people want their lives to be consonant with reality, for them not to be, as we say, 'out of true'. Someone with a different vision – who sees the world as ordered in accord with a divine purpose, say, or as nothing but a complex of physical particles – will want to live in a different way. Or, at any rate, will not feel drawn to cultivate the virtues that I identified. Why would a person want to cultivate the humility that goes with appreciation of the mystery of the world if he or she doesn't recognize any mystery? Why would people who think the natural world was created as raw material for their benefit wish to encourage a sense of convergence with it?

Notice that I speak of a person with a certain vision of the world wanting, wishing, or being drawn to cultivate certain virtues and live in a certain way. I do not speak of what, given this vision, one *ought* to do. There is no question here of deducing from a description of the world conclusions about what you are obliged to do and feel. But this is not because it is, instead, a matter of 'choice' or 'decision' how, in the light of a vision of the way of things, the good life is to be determined. Once more the ancients had it right in their insistence that, once the world figures for you in a clear vision, you are bound to be drawn to living in a certain way. The question of how you 'ought' to respond doesn't arise for you: there is no smorgasbord before you of competing virtues to choose between. How, for instance, could you experience the world as mysterious without wanting to foster the humility that flows from appreciation of the limits of knowledge?

So, someone who shares the vision of the world that I proposed will want to cultivate the virtues I identified. But, conversely, someone who is already attracted to those virtues will want the world to be the one that figures in this vision. This is because we need to think that the world is receptive or hospitable to the virtues we embrace. Imagine how it would be for a man wedded to the samurai virtue of unquestioning readiness to die for one's master to find himself plonked down into the modern social world, one without any scope for the exercise of such virtues. We can commit to cultivating virtues that attract us only if we regard the world as one in which a life guided by them could flourish. The cultivation of happiness, in the sense developed in Chapter 6, is only a virtue in a world that is not fixed and static, in which vigour, imagination and initiative find a response and a reward.

That the world be seen as hospitable to the exercise of virtues helps to explain why, in the ancient traditions I referred to, great importance is attached to exemplary figures – the consummate persons, sages and enlightened persons whom we met earlier. In Buddhism, for example, the nearest analogue to faith is, in Pali, *saddhā*. But this refers, not to blind acceptance of some doctrine, rather to confidence or trust in, above all, the Buddha himself. The figure of the Buddha is walking confirmation that a life of virtue is a flourishing one – confirmation, therefore, that the world is a place in which certain virtues make for a life that is both feasible and good. More generally, the exemplary figures of various traditions give people confidence that, in embracing the virtues they do, they are not deceiving themselves about the character of the world in which these virtues are to be exercised.

It is not just the importance of exemplary figures that is explained by the twinned desires for the cultivation of certain virtues and for the world to be of a certain kind. So is the importance of certain experiences – those that express the virtues and evoke a vision of the world. These experiences furnished the ancient literatures with their preferred metaphors and images. Above all, it is the experience of sunlight glittering on the surface of water whose importance is implied. For this experience, in its beauty, is itself confirmation that our twinned desires will be realized. To experience the phenomenon as beautiful is to sense that it is expressive of virtues and that the world it evokes is an appropriate arena in which to exercise them.

To experience the sun on the sea in this way is inspiring, for it is an acquaintance with all three of the dimensions of the ancient conception of the good life – beauty, goodness, and truth. That it is an inspiring, indeed exhilarating experience was emphasized by vitalists, like D.H. Lawrence. We're now able to offer an explanation of this exhilaration that goes deeper than the tonic effect of sun and sea on a person's skin, mood and energy level.

Friedrich Nietzsche was a lover of the sun and sea, spending a lot of time in the north of Italy in the years before the mental and physical collapse from which he never recovered. The pleasures of sunlight and water were, for him, among those 'little things' whose importance in the good life has been ignored by religion and philosophy. Nietzsche is here trying to bring philosophy down to earth, back to the body. But he did not intend to commit the opposite error to that of religious moralists and ignore the spiritual in favour of a crude materialism. The human spirit does not float above the sensual and the bodily, but we may still aspire to 'the spiritualization and augmentation of the senses'. This spiritualization may occur through art, or through heightened experiences of the world around us. In the enjoyment of sunlight reflected by water, Nietzsche found the 'ever-greater pleasure and warmth to the "things of this world"' that he sought. Here is a pleasure that testifies to the human capacity to 'transfigure' experience of the ordinary into 'the best we have in the way of spirit'.

Just such a transfiguration, surely, is being recorded by the poet Rebecca Hubbard when she describes how, looking at the reflection of reeds in the water she is swimming through, she experiences it as 'a hint, an awakening to to what is usually contained and concealed within forms – energy, movement, light, life force'.

Perhaps the last word should be left to a thinker more associated than any other with the idea of a life force, and with the cult of 'Life' at the beginning of the last century. During Henri Bergson's lectures at the Collège de France in the years before the First World War, it is reported that women would swoon at his erotically charged descriptions of an *élan vital* that coursed through and penetrated the universe and that we should embrace in our own lives. The world that Bergson goes on to describe is not unlike the one I characterized as a perspectival whole of experience. It is a world of spontaneous movement, a 'continual flowing', that gets artificially carved up into discrete objects through 'the work of the intellect'. Bergson then proceeds to describe the stirring effect – the kind it perhaps had on the women at his lectures – that experiencing the world in this way should have. What had been 'frozen in our perception', he writes, becomes 'warmed and set in motion. Everything comes to life around us'. We sense 'a great impulse carr[ying] things along ... We are more fully alive'.

The feeling of vitality, vigour and a life enhanced that certain experiences afford us is grounded, then, in an integrated vision of the world and our own being. Life in the vitalist sense takes its place within the wider economy of the good life. Bergson spent most of his time in Paris, but it's nice to imagine that it was the sight of sunlight reflected by flowing water – perhaps the sea Monet painted at Le Havre – that made the world, like himself, feel 'more fully alive'.

SOURCES AND NOTES

References are in the same order in which the sources were cited in each chapter

1 The Sun and the Sea

Norman Douglas, *Siren Land*, quoted in Alan Ross, *Reflections on Blue Water*, London: Faber & Faber, 2012, Kindle ed., loc.3263; Llewelyn Powys, quoted in Rachel Carson, *The Sea around Us*, Oxford: Oxford University Press, 1989, p.131; the 'poetic champion' of surfing is Drew Campion, *The Book of Waves*, Lanham, MD: Roberts Rinehart, 1991; Scott Fitzgerald and Edward Carpenter, quoted in Robert Mighall, *Sunshine: One Man's Search for Happiness,* London: John Murray, 2008, pp.106, 53; Carl Nielsen, see Notes to Erik Tuxen's 1952 recording of the Helios Overture; John Ruskin, *Modern Painters*, London: Deutsch, 1987, pp.136-7, 147; Arthur Schopenhauer, *The World as Will and Representation* Vol I, New York: Dover, 1969, pp.199-200; T.S. Eliot, 'East Coker', *Collected Poems* 1909-62, London: Faber & Faber, 1974, p.203; Carson, *The Sea around Us*, p.23; D.H. Lawrence, *Sea and Sardinia*, New York: Seltzer, 1921, Kindle ed., locs. 505, 693; Henri Matisse, quoted in Hilary Spurling, *Matisse the Master: A Life of Henri Matisse* Vol 2, London: Hamish Hamilton, 2005, pp.142, 320; the Ischia hermit is quoted in Ross, *Reflections on Blue Water*, loc.3032; Ralph Waldo Emerson, 'Nature 1844', in his *Essays and English Traits*, New York: Collier 1909-14, p.2; Lawrence, 'The Sea', *The Complete Poems of D.H. Lawrence*, Ware: Wordsworth Editions, 1994, p.147.

2 Life and Illumination

The Spanish philosopher was Miguel de Unamuno, *Tragic Sense of Life*, New York: Dover, 1954, p.115; Lawrence, *The Selected Letters of D.H. Lawrence*, Cambridge: Cambridge University Press, 1997, p.53; Friedrich

Nietzsche, *Thus Spoke Zarathustra*, Oxford: Oxford University Press, 2005, pp.107-8, 287; Lawrence, 'Sun', *Complete Short Stories* Vol 2, London: Heinemann, 1955, pp.533ff; Nietzsche, *Ecce Homo, Basic Writings of Nietzsche*, New York: Modern Library, 1968, p.712; for Socrates on the unity of knowledge and virtue, see Plato's *Protagoras*, 357ff.; the Buddhist remarks on beauty are from the *Digha Nikaya* (Long Discourses of the Buddha), Sutta 26, and the *Therigatha* (Verses of the Female Elders), §363; *Buddhism without Beliefs* is the title of a book by Stephen Batchelor, London: Bloomsbury, 1998; the remark on Shinto is from Thomas Kasulis, *Shinto: The Way Home*, Honolulu: University of Hawai'i Press, 2004, p.32; the *Daodejing* (Chapters 1 and 56) exists in many translations, eg, Philip Ivanoe's, Indianapolis, IN: Hackett, 2002; Dōgen, *Shobogenzo* Vol 2, London: Windbell, Ch 22.3; Plato, *Republic*, 506e, 507c, 516a; on 'the Buddha's light' and the 'quicksilver universe', see Paul Williams, *Mahayana Buddhism*, London: Routledge, 1989, pp.122-3; Dōgen's remark on dewdrops is from *Moon in a Dewdrop: Writings of Zen Master Dōgen*, New York: North Point Press, p.71; Zhuangzi's remark on mind and water is in A.C. Graham, *Chuang-Tzu: The Inner Chapters*, Indianapolis, IN: Hackett, 2001, p.266.

3 **Beauty and Radiance**

Plato, *Symposium*, 211b ff; André Gide, *The Immoralist*, London: Penguin, 1960, p.143; Schopenhauer, *The World as Will and Representation*, Vol 2 Ch 46 and Vol 1 §38; St Thomas Aquinas, *Philosophical Texts*, London: Oxford University Press, 1956, pp.77-79; the 'historian of the late middle ages' is Johan Huizinga, *The Waning of the Middle Ages*, London: Penguin, 2001, p.258; the remark on sunlight and God is from Dionysius the Areopagite, *On the Divine Names*, Berwick, ME: Ibis, 2004, p.92; James Joyce, *A Portrait of the Artist as a Young Man*, London: Penguin, 1977, p.288; Aquinas, *Philosophical Texts*, p.78; George Eliot and Henry James as quoted in Nancy Etcoff, *The Survival of the Prettiest*, London: Abacus, 2000, p.258.

4 'In Praise of Shadows'

Junichirō Tanizaki, *In Praise of Shadows*, London: Vintage, 2001; Kamo no Chōmei, in *Sources of Japanese Tradition* Vol 1, New York: Columbia University Press, 2001, p.387; on *wabi*, see Haga Kōshiro, in Nancy Hume ed., *Japanese Aesthetics and Culture*, Albany, NY: SUNY Press, 1995, p.249; Leonardo da Vinci, *A Treatise on Painting*, New York: Dover, 2005, p.71; Sōetsu Yanagi, *The Unknown Craftsman: A Japanese Insight into Beauty*, Tokyo: Kodansha, 1972, p.148; Motoori Norinaga, quoted in Richard Pilgrim, *Buddhism and the Arts of Japan*, Chambersburg, PA: Anima, 1993, p.10; Charles Baudelaire, 'Critical method', in C. Harrison and P. Wood eds., *Art in Theory* 1815-1900, Oxford: Blackwell, 1998, p.487.

5 Expression

The Sri Lankan teacher is Godwin Samararatne, *A Beautiful Way of Living*, Kandy: Buddhist Publication Society, 2011, p.62; on 'the sign of the beautiful', see the *Samyutta Nikaya* (Connected Discourses of the Buddha), Sutta 46 and Buddhaghosa, *The Path of Purification*, Kandy: Buddhist Publication Society, 1991, n. 14 p.752; Ludwig Wittgenstein, *Philosophical Investigations*, London: Macmillan, 1969, p.178; on the Buddha's beauty, see Asvaghosa, *Buddha-Karita* in *Buddhist Mahayana Texts*, Oxford: Oxford University Press, 1894, Book III; on the Sri Lankan monks, see Jeffrey Samuels, *Attracting the Heart*, Honolulu: University of Hawai'i Press, 2010, pp.xxiv, 78-9; on Andy Goldsworthy, see David Macauley, *Elemental Philosophy*, Albany, NY: SUNY Press, 2010, p.250; Claude Monet, quoted in Caroline Holmes, *Monet at Giverny*, London: Cassell, 2001, p.42.

6 Happiness

On 'profound *de*', see *Daodejing*, Ch 65; Robert Mighall, *Sunshine*, p.148; Vincent Van Gogh, *The Letters of Vincent Van Gogh*, London: Fontana, 1967, p.316; Nietzsche, *Thus Spoke Zarathustra*, Introduction, p.xiii; Lawrence, 'Sun-women', *The Complete Poems of D.H. Lawrence*, p.439; C.P. Cavafy, 'Morning sea', *The Collected Poems*, Oxford: Oxford University Press, 2007, p.69; J.W. von Goethe, *The Flight to Italy*, Oxford: Oxford University Press, 1999, p.86; Matthew Arnold, 'Empedocles', *Oxford Book of English Verse*, Oxford: Oxford University Press, 1939, p.923; Ludwig Wittgenstein, *Tractatus Logico-Philosophicus*, London: Routledge, 1988, §6.43; Elizabeth Bishop, 'Pleasure seas', *Poems*, London: Chatto & Windus, 2011, p.279; Aristotle, *Nicomachean Ethics*, 1102a.

7 Spontaneity

On Confucius and water, see Confucius, *The Analects*, IX.17 and *Mencius*, IVB.18; on Daoism, water and spontaneity, see *Daodejing*, Chs 8, 25, 34, 55, Zhuangzi, *Chuang-Tzu: The Inner Chapters*, Chs 5, 19, with A.C. Graham's Introduction, p.14, and Sarah Allan, *The Way of Water and Sprouts of Virtue*, Albany, NY: SUNY Press.

8 Convergence with Nature

Thomas Bernhard, *Wittgenstein's Nephew: A Friendship*, London: Vintage, 1992, p.62; G.W.F. Hegel, *Phenomenology of Spirit*, Oxford: Oxford University Press, 1977, c. p.130; Francis Bacon, *The New Organum and Related Writings*, Indianapolis, IN: Bobbs-Merrill, 1969, p.19; the Marxist historian is quoted in John Passmore, *Man's Responsibility for Nature*, London: Duckworth, 1980, pp.24-5; on convergence with nature generally, see David E. Cooper, *Convergence with Nature: A Daoist Perspective*, Dartington: Green Books, 2012; on Ruskin on Turner, see Eric Shaner, 'The Sun is God', in E. Joll et al eds., *The Oxford Companion to J.W.M. Turner*, Oxford: Oxford University

Press, 2001, p.320; on the duck skulls, see Tim Birkhead, *The Wisdom of Birds*, London: Bloomsbury, 2008, p.189; the 'perceptive essay' on Turner is by Jonathan Crary, 'The Blinding Light', in *J.W.M. Turner: The Sun is God*, London: Tate Gallery, 2000, p.24; Maurice Merleau-Ponty, 'Eye and Mind', in *Merleau-Ponty: Basic Writings*, London: Routledge, 2004, p.319; Roger Deakin, *Notes from Walnut Tree Farm*, London: Penguin, 2009, p.283; the surfer is described in Drew Kampion, *The Lost Coast: Stories from the Surf*, Salt Lake City, UT: Gibbs Smith, 2007, Kindle ed., loc.1716; Albert Camus, *Summer in Algiers*, London: Penguin, 2005, pp.3, 12, 49, 53; on Axel Munthe, see Ross, *Reflections on Water*, locs. 776ff.

9 Humility

Kenkō, *Essays in Idleness*, New York: Columbia University Press, 1967, pp.70, 137, 164; the 'Japanese-American writer' is Yuriko Saito, 'Japanese Aesthetics', *A Companion to Aesthetics*, Oxford: Wiley-Blackwell, 2009, p.386; Yanagi, *The Unknown Craftsman*, p.188; on humility, Iris Murdoch's 'selfless respect' etc., see David E. Cooper, *The Measure of Things: Humanism, Humility and Mystery*, Oxford: Oxford University Press, 2002; on 'ways' in East Asian culture, see Graham Parkes, 'Japanese Aesthetics', *Stanford Encyclopedia of Philosophy*, 2005, and H.E. Davey, *The Japanese Way of the Artist*, Berkeley, CA: Stone Bridge, 2012, Kindle ed., loc. 217 for comment on Japanese calligrapher; on the tea ceremony and Sen no Rikyū, see *Sources of Japanese Tradition*, pp.395ff, Kakuzo Okakura, *The Way of Tea*, Tokyo: Kodansha, 1989, p.24, and Yanagi, *The Unknown Craftsman*, p.179; Alain de Botton, *The Architecture of Happiness*, London: Penguin, 2006, p.235; for Ryōkan, see *One Robe, One Bowl: The Zen Poetry of Ryōkan*, New York: Weatherhill, 1977.

10 Epiphanies

The *Bhagavad Gita*, Ch.11; *Heraclitus: The Cosmic Fragments*, Cambridge: Cambridge University Press, 1970; Jean-Paul Sartre, *Nausea*, London: Penguin, 1965, pp.182ff; on gardens as epiphanies, see David E. Cooper, *A Philosophy of Gardens*, Oxford: Oxford University Press, 2006; Tan Twan Eng, *The Garden of Evening Mists*, London: Canongate, 2013, p.163; for the Wordsworth poems, see *William Wordsworth: A Critical Edition of the Major Works*, Oxford: Oxford University Press, 1984; Tan Twan Eng, *The Garden of Evening Mists*, p.27.

11 Aspects of the World

The Diamond Sutra, Santa Barbara, CA: Concord Grove, 1983, p.28; the description of the Mahayana view is Paul Williams', *Mahayana Buddhism*, p.123; F.H. Bradley, *Appearance and Reality*, Oxford: Oxford University Press, 1930, pp.409, 465; the description of the Solent is Philip Hoare's, *The Sea Inside*, London: Fourth Estate, 2013, Kindle ed., loc.169f; Plotinus, *The Enneads*, London: Penguin, 1991, V.3.12; on Shankara, see S. Radhakrishnan, *Indian Philosophy* Vol 2, Oxford: Oxford University Press, 1923, p.607; Dōgen, *Moon in a Dewdrop*, p.71; Merleau-Ponty, quoted and paraphrased in David Abram, *The Spell of the Sensuous*, New York: Vintage, 1996, pp.54ff, 68; for 'Zen telegrams', see David Macauley, *Elemental Philosophy*, p.246, and for 'ineffable glances', see Ralph Waldo Emerson, 'Nature 1844', p.2; Merleau-Ponty, 'Cézanne's doubt', *Basic Writings*, pp.277-8; *Daodejing,* Ch 25.

12 World, Experience, Mystery

William James, 'Pragmatism and Humanism', *The Writings of William James*, Chicago: University of Chicago Press, 1977, pp.451ff; Bradley, *Appearance and Reality*, p.403; for Nietzsche's mosquito, see *Philosophy and Truth: Selections from Nietzsche's Notebooks of the Early 1870s*, Atlantic Highlands, NJ: Humanities, 1979, pp.79-80; Schopenhauer, *The World as Will and Representation* Vol 1 §99; D.T. Suzuki, *Essays on Zen*

Buddhism Vol III, London: Luzac, 1934, pp.240, 250; Dōgen, *Shobogenzo* Vol 2 Ch 3.19; for 'double exposure', see Suzuki, *Essays in Zen Buddhism* Vol III, p.256.

13 Sun and Moon

D.T. Suzuki, *Zen and Japanese Culture*, Princeton, NJ: Princeton University Press, 1959, p.393; Erazim Kohák, *The Embers and the Stars*, Chicago: Chicago University Press, 1984, pp.32ff; on Leonardo's *sfumato*, see John Danvers, *Agents of Uncertainty*, New York: Rodopi, 2012, p.158; on Descartes and the sun, see Jonathan Crary, 'The blinding light', p.23; Elizabeth Bishop, 'Pleasure seas', *Poems*, p.279.

14 Life

Martin Heidegger, *Nietzsche* Vol 1, London: Routledge, 1981, pp.196-98; Stendhal, *Love*, London: Penguin, 1975, n.1 p.66; Nietzsche, *The Will to Power*, New York: Vintage, 1968, §820; Rebecca Hubbard, author of *The Garden of Shadow and Delight*, Gwynned: Cinnamon, 2014, in personal communication; Henri Bergson, 'The Perception of Change', *Bergson: Key Writings*, London: Continuum, 2002, p.266.

THE AUTHOR

David E. Cooper is a philosopher and the author of many books, including *World Philosophies: An Historical Introduction*, *The Measure of Things: Humanism, Humility and Mystery*, *A Philosophy of Gardens*, and *Convergence with Nature: A Daoist Perspective*. (For a fuller list, visit Amazon's David E. Cooper page). Until 2009 he was Professor of Philosophy at Durham University, and has been a Visiting Professor in several countries, including the USA, Canada, Sri Lanka, Malta and South Africa. He now divides his time between writing and his work as the Secretary and a Trustee of the charity Project Sri Lanka (http://www.projectsrilanka.org.uk). He is currently writing a book - on music and nature - that brings together two of his main enthusiasms. He lives in Northumberland.